EVERYDAY
Magic

EVERYDAY
Magic

Nevill Drury

ROBERT HALE · LONDON

© *Nevill Drury 2002*
Original edition published by Simon & Schuster (Australia) Pty Ltd
First published in Great Britain 2002

ISBN 0 7090 7128 0

Robert Hale Limited
Clerkenwell House
Clerkenwell Green
London EC1R 0HT

A catalogue record for this book is available
from the British Library

2 4 6 8 10 9 7 5 3 1

Printed by
St Edmundsbury Press, Bury St Edmunds
and bound by
Woolnough Bookbinding Limited, Irthlingborough

For me the world is weird because it is stupendous,
awesome, mysterious, unfathomable;
my interest has been to convince you
that you must assume responsibility for being here,
in this marvellous world ...
in this marvellous time.

YAQUI SHAMAN DON JUAN, SPEAKING WITH
CARLOS CASTANEDA
(from *Journey to Ixtlan*)

CONTENTS

PREFACE

Magic offers us a special way of approaching our everyday lives. This book draws on magical ideas and practices from several different wisdom traditions, including the Kabbalah, Wicca and Goddess spirituality, alchemy, shamanism and the Tarot. I have tried to write it in a way that is accessible and easy to read, but also to present magic in a way which shows its full visionary potential.

It is easy to trivialise the magical arts and reduce them simply to a method of self-gain and advancement. What I have endeavoured to do here is to present the magical paths in a broader light, to show how they offer a way of personal transformation which extends beyond the individual into a much broader context. Certainly, magic can bring us prosperity and success with our own individual aspirations, but real magic is much more than this. Real magic helps restore our sense of the sacred. It changes the way we view the world and the way we relate to our fellow travellers. It shows us

1

how we can explore the spiritual potential we all have within us, and it shows us how to respect and revere the cyclic and spiritual forces of Nature.

I have tried, therefore, to produce something more than just a standard self-help book. I have included numerous magical techniques and visualisations throughout the text, so on one level it certainly is a practical approach to developing magical awareness. But I am also hoping here to help recover that sense of wonder and enchantment which is so easily lost in this modern world of advanced technology and mechanistic complexity. To that extent I hope you will find some inspirational elements in here as well.

This book shows how magic can help us attune ourselves to our psychic and spiritual depths − to discover the gods and goddesses within. The magical traditions remind us that as individual human beings we are all connected to the Universal Spirit. It is our destiny to discover the sacred bonds which connect us with the Universe and to explore our place within the larger scheme of things. So magic is really a visionary approach to the world we live in. If we can bring this principle into our normal everyday lives we will surely be practising *everyday magic*.

Nevill Drury

INTRODUCTION

If we pause to reflect for a moment, and ask a couple of fundamental questions about our own life on the planet – why are we here? what is the ultimate nature of our existence? – we will be forced to concede that our lives are really a complete mystery. If we were to answer the questions honestly, the truth is *we really don't know*. And yet so much of our daily life is based on the notion of a definite and specific physical reality – the reality of the world we live in, the world we experience. We know how we like to look and dress and engage with other people. We know the sort of work we do, the car we drive, the music we listen to. We know which colours we like, our favourite foods in a restaurant. Our ability to utilise computer technology and the ever-expanding potentials of the Internet are, by now, central to our personal effectiveness and even our sense of self-esteem. Key up a website address and connect immediately. Press a button and achieve an immediate outcome. Scan an image – any image – and capture it in your hard drive. For most of us, daily life is not only becoming faster and increasingly more efficient but also more *tangible*. We think and act as if we are in total control; we believe we know totally who we are and where we are going.

But clearly this isn't the case. How did we come to such an unwarranted conclusion?

Obviously, we have to operate on the basis that our existence is real. If we didn't, we would in all likelihood go mad. When we sit down on a chair we feel it is solid. We know that if we collide at speed with a brick wall we will cause serious injury to ourselves, perhaps even death. The physical experiences with which we engage every day reinforce the formula *physical = real*. But how real is real? How substantial is substance? How specific and distinct are material objects, our bodies included? And are there other realms of awareness beyond the purely physical?

Although this book is about magic, and we will soon be focusing specifically on the magical traditions themselves, the answer which emerges in response to these questions is very much a matter of science. The fact is, according to the now well-established paradigms of quantum physics – which in turn take science to its furthest frontier – we are not as solid as we think we are. In a structural sense, as sentient human beings alive on planet Earth, each one of us can be regarded as a unique fusion of energy and form, and from a physical perspective each of our bodies contains more space than substance. Which is not so much a put-down as simply a reflection on how things are – or appear to be.

Physical reality and the disappearing universe

Most of us, in drawing on the apparent evidence of our senses, still continue to hold to the so-called Newtonian–Cartesian model of the universe, which is based on the ideas of the pioneering thinkers Isaac Newton and René Descartes. In this model the basic elements of the material universe are regarded as solid and ultimately indestructible. Descartes believed that mind and matter were intrinsically separate – that matter was inert, and that the universe was objectively real, independent of the process of observation. This has been called the mechanistic world-view.

However, we now know, through our understanding of quantum physics, that at the subatomic level, physical matter is often wave-like and in a state of flux, and that the apparently solid foundations of the physical world are not as solid as we might have thought. The well-known Czech psychiatrist and consciousness researcher Dr Stanislav Grof believes that the authority of the mechanistic world-view – the view that the world is intrinsically solid – began to dissolve when scientists realised that atoms were essentially empty. As Dr Grof has written: 'In subatomic analysis, solid Newtonian matter disappeared. What remained were activity, form, abstract order and pattern. In the words of the famous mathematician and physicist Sir James Jeans, the universe began to look less like a machine and more like a thought system.'[1]

Quantum physics has thus led to a completely new way of viewing our everyday existence. Moreover, it has had profound implications for the way we consider human consciousness – and, by extension, the various realms of magical

5

awareness. Quantum physics has shown that subatomic particles remain in a state of continuous flux: there are no fixed or separate building blocks in the known universe. Quantum physicist Dr David Bohm, who worked with Einstein, has also suggested that mind (or consciousness) appears to be an innate property of matter.[2]

The psychological implications of quantum physics are also fascinating. American physicist Danah Zohar relates the principles of quantum mechanics directly to an understanding of the human condition and raises the curious issue that on a physical level the individual organism – the personal 'self' or identity we are so sure of – is subject to continual change. It is an intriguing fact, for example, that the neurones in the brain and the cells of the human body are entirely renewed every seven years. So where, Zohar asks, does this leave our sense of self and individuality? Indeed, if individual people are real, what is it that holds them together? Each of us is an organism made up of billions of cells, with each cell in some sense possessing a life of its own. Within our brains alone, some 10 000 million neurones contribute to the rich tapestry of our mental life. And yet if our brains consist of all those myriad neurones, how does the idea of a 'person' actually emerge and how tangible is that person's existence?

Danah Zohar's conclusion is that people, like subatomic matter, sometimes behave like particles while on other occasions they behave more like waves, and that both states can be equally possible, depending on the situation. What we regard as our individuality – our sense of separateness, our uniqueness as a person – is equivalent to the apparent separateness of a particle, whereas the way we interrelate with others, and with the world as a whole, has more the characteristic of a wave. If we consider the human being from the perspective of quantum theory – that is, as a quantum self – both aspects emerge. Seen this way, Zohar says: 'the *quantum* self is simply a more fluid self, changing and evolving at every moment, now separating into sub-selves, now reuniting into a larger self. It ebbs and flows, but always in some sense[is] being itself ...'3

This is very much an energy-based model of what it means to be human. Clearly, without a sense of wholeness there is no sense of self. And yet we all know from our own experiences in the physical world that human consciousness is characterised by a sense of unbroken wholeness and continuity which provides us with a sense of cohesion in daily life. Zohar believes that, in the final analysis, quantum theory leads us towards the realisation that consciousness is either a property of matter or that consciousness and matter arise together from the same source. And, inevitably, all sentient beings are ultimately connected and share a common destiny on the planet.

But what has the nature of human life and physical reality got to do with magic? The answer is this: magic proposes an energy-based view of human existence which asserts that our individual sense of 'reality' depends directly on our level of conscious awareness. As we will see, physical space and magical space belong in the same universe and are essentially reflections of one another.

Magic is real – take that quantum leap

Now that we have challenged our familiar notions of everyday physical reality, let's compare the world of magic with the world of quantum physics.

As we have seen, according to the findings of quantum physics, matter is not intrinsically solid but consists primarily of space, and objects we assume are solid actually exhibit the characteristics of waves. Quantum physics emphasises a web of relationships rather than notions of individual separateness, leading us to the view that at a primal-energy level all things in the known universe are interconnected. As we have noted, some quantum physicists also believe consciousness is a property of matter itself. According to this view, the universe is basically *alive*.

The fascinating thing about all this is that in many ways the paradigms of magic and quantum physics actually support each other. Since Palaeolithic times, shamans – the world's earliest practitioners of visionary magic – have believed that all things in the known universe are interconnected on a spiritual or energetic level and that the world is intrinsically alive. For shamans generally (and shamans are still found in hunter-gatherer cultures across the planet) the universal life-force is revered as sacred, and the path of true meaning is found by exploring a web of sacred interrelationships.

Magicians themselves are travellers in deep space – not the outer space of the physicist or astronomer but the inner space of the mystic. By exploring trance states and mystical states of consciousness, shamans in all eras of recorded culture have learned to explore the pulse of human existence. And their conclusion has been essentially the same as that of the quantum physicist: *the cosmos extends into infinite space in all directions, the universe is subject to continual flux and change – characterised by the universal flow of life-energy – and everything we experience as human beings is part of a universal flow of energy.*

Magicians in all traditions and cultures also recognise the

essential unity of all things and have always been aware that conscious intelligence is innate to the very structure of the universe. Magicians know that everything in the material world is interconnected in an energetic sense. Indeed, magic wouldn't work if it wasn't. For, as we will see later in this book, magic works fundamentally on an energetic level. And because energy can be shaped by thought – by focusing the conscious will – we can then open our awareness to any and all possibilities envisaged by the human imagination. This is where magic has its basic strength and can play an important role in our everyday lives. This is our starting point for understanding the potentials of everyday magic.

A central theme of this book is that magic is an approach to life which is both specific and indeterminate, for it is focused in an individual sense but must always remain open-ended in a universal sense. All magicians recognise that the universe is finally mysterious, that the ultimate sacred reality is beyond the scope of our limited human understanding. However, throughout history there have been different metaphysical ways of addressing the Great Mystery, of clothing it in symbols and sacred rituals to help us grasp the core truths of its transcendental nature and give it more tangible and specific meaning. This, I believe, is the relevance of magic today. Far from equating magic with superstition and illusion, which is how many people continue to regard it, real magic – *authentic* magic – is based on a deep understanding of the sacred and symbolic realities which provide meaning in the world. And nothing could be more real than that.

*

CHAPTER ONE

Magic, symbol and image

All forms of magic make use of sacred symbols to convey spiritual meaning. The magical traditions acknowledge that as human beings we cannot deal on an everyday level with something which is forever abstract and transcendent, however profound it may be in the ultimate sense. And so all of the major magical traditions – the various approaches which, taken together, make up what is often referred to as the Western esoteric tradition – employ a variety of symbols and different forms of spiritual practice to approach the Great Mystery found at the very heart of life itself.

For most practitioners who take magic seriously, the magical quest is pursued in a spirit of reverence and humility. Undoubtedly there have been magicians who have gained a reputation for their arrogance and greed in pursuit of spiritual power, however misguided this may be in the

ultimate scheme of things. But the genuine magical quest
has to do with the principle of recognising the deeply spiritual nature of all things, and acknowledging that each of us
as fellow human beings has a contribution to make and a
role to play. Essentially, magic is about the transformation of
both ourselves and the world in which we live.

There are several important spiritual traditions which contribute collectively to the magical world-view. What I would
like to describe here are the central symbolic features presented by each of these traditions, as contributions to what we can
regard as a perennial wisdom path for the new millennium.
Because this is not a history book so much as an overview of
different magical and symbolic ways of relating to the world, I
do not intend to weigh this commentary down with academic
details. For those readers who are interested, I have included a
lengthy reading list at the back of this book.

The major magical traditions

The major magical traditions – the traditions which have
contributed most substantially to our understanding of
magical consciousness – are as follows:

* the Kabbalah
* the Major Arcana of the Tarot
* Alchemy
* Wicca and Goddess spirituality
* Shamanism

The Kabbalah

The Kabbalah is the name given to the sacred tradition of
Jewish mysticism. The word *kabbalah* itself translates as

'from mouth to ear' and refers to a secret, oral tradition. The Kabbalah is generally regarded as a mystical interpretation of the Torah, the first five books of the Old Testament, although the principal text of the Kabbalah – the *Zohar* – was not written down until the 13th century, when it was compiled by a Spanish mystic named Moses de Leon. Nevertheless, the Kabbalah is probably as ancient as the Old Testament Jewish tradition itself. Many scholars believe that the Book of Genesis and its account of the Seven Days of Creation cannot be truly understood without an awareness of the spiritual themes of the Kabbalah, for it is in the Kabbalistic teachings that an effort is made to explain the symbolic process of divine creation and the cosmological origins of the universe.

The Kabbalistic explanation of the creation of the universe is based on a wonderful and very profound theme – the idea of Spirit, or infinite formlessness, gradually becoming more manifest, producing a succession of different levels of mystical reality before finally giving rise to the physical world as we know it.

In a sense this is not so different from the quantum concept of the universe we mentioned earlier – the idea that physical matter appears to contain the potentials for consciousness within its very structure, even though matter itself consists mostly of space. Expressed another way we can say that, according to the Kabbalah, before the world was formed, the universe consisted of infinite sacred energy (known variously in the Kabbalah as *En-Sof, Ain Soph* or *Ain Soph Aur*) and this sacred energy gradually acquired a more tangible outer form by manifesting through different levels of being. This process happened phase by phase – in the Kabbalah it is said that a bolt of lightning, representing the life-force, descended through ten different levels on the Tree of Life. These ten levels on the Tree are known as *sephiroth* ('energy-essences' or 'spheres'). They are symbolic and are not meant to be taken literally. The first three sephiroth represent the Trinity and remain pure and transcendent, unsullied by the descent of Infinite Spirit into the finite world of physical matter. The next seven sephiroth represent the Seven Days of Creation. Between the Trinity and the manifested world of Creation lies the Abyss, a level clearly demarcated on the Tree to convey the idea of the 'Fall of Spirit' from infinite to finite awareness.

According to the Kabbalah, the mystical universe is sustained by the utterance of the Holy Names of God, and the ten spheres upon the Tree of Life are none other than 'the creative names which God called into the world, the names which He gave to Himself'.[1]

In the *Zohar* we read:

In the Beginning, when the will of the King began to take effect, he engraved signs into the divine aura. A dark flame sprang forth from the innermost recess of the mystery of the Infinite, *En-Sof* [*Ain Soph Aur*] like a fog which forms out of the formless, enclosed in the ring of this aura, neither white nor black, neither red nor green, and of no colour whatever. But when this flame began to assume size and extension it produced radiant colours. For in the innermost centre of the flame a well sprang forth from which flames poured upon everything below, hidden in the mysterious secrets of *En-Sof.* The well broke through, and yet did not entirely break through, the ethereal aura which surrounded it. It was entirely unrecognisable until under the impact of its breakthrough a hidden supernal point shone forth. Beyond this point nothing may be known or understood, and therefore it is called *Reshith*, that is 'Beginning', the first word of Creation.[2]

These words are endeavouring to describe a process which in the ultimate sense cannot really be described, for we are dealing here with the Great Mystery – the creation of the world out of formlessness. Nevertheless, as this text describes, with the manifestation of the first spark of Creation the universe gradually came into existence. In the Kabbalah the ten levels of Creation are as follows: **Kether**, the Crown, or first point of Creation; **Chokmah**, Wisdom (the Father); **Binah**, Understanding (the Mother); **Chesed**, Mercy; **Geburah**, Severity, or Strength; **Tiphareth**, Beauty, or Harmony (the Son); **Netzach**, Victory; **Hod**, Splendour; **Yesod**, the Foundation; **Malkuth**, Kingdom, or Earth (the Daughter). These ten spheres of consciousness also reside as spheres or spiritual centres within the body of the archetypal human being, known by the Jews as Adam Kadmon. Diagrams depicting these spheres position them in the body in a similar way to the chakras of Indian yoga (see also Chapter Four). The symbolic concept of these archetypal spheres conveys the idea that by knowing ourselves in the fullest mystical sense, we also come to know God, because ultimately there is only one supreme reality in the universe. This same concept later entered the Western mystical tradition through the expression 'As above, so below' – meaning that every human being contains the sacred potentials and divine life-force of the whole universe.

In more recent times the Tree of Life has been used in the Western magical tradition as a type of universal framework of 'mythic' consciousness. It has become possible – although

Orthodox Jewish Kabbalists no doubt frown at the idea – to map other mythologies upon the Tree of Life by assigning them to the different spiritual 'spheres'. Here we also encounter the idea that the gods and goddesses of different spiritual traditions are somehow equivalent to each other – cultural variables on an archetypal theme. For example, many practising magicians locate the gods and goddesses of ancient Greece and Rome upon the Tree, as well as those from ancient Egypt and other early civilisations. When we consider the Tree of Life in this 'mythological' way – and this is certainly the way it is now represented in the Western esoteric tradition – the ten spheres of consciousness are as follows.

KETHER

This stage of consciousness represents Ultimate Reality – the first spark of Creation which comes forth from beyond the veils of non-existence. Kether represents sublime spiritual transcendence.

CHOKMAH

This is the sphere of wisdom, represented by the Great Father. Cosmologically he provides the spark of life which enters the womb of the Great Mother. The union of the Great Father and the Great Mother then produces all the images and forms of Creation.

BINAH

Binah represents the Great Mother in all her mythological aspects. In different world mythologies she is regarded as the Mother of Creation and for this reason she is often the wife of the ruler of the manifested universe. For example, in

Greek mythology Demeter is the wife of Zeus, and in the corresponding Roman mythology Ceres is the wife of Jupiter.

CHESED

Associated with Zeus and Jupiter, Chesed represents the peaceful face of the ruler of the universe and the qualities of divine mercy and majesty. Chesed is protective and tends to reinforce and consolidate the forces of Creation. In the sphere of Chesed, Jupiter is shown seated upon his throne. Here he surveys his kingdom – the entire manifested universe.

GEBURAH

Associated with Mars, traditionally a god of war, Geburah represents severity and justice. The destructive energies of this sphere are intended as a purging, cleansing force and are positive in their application.

TIPHARETH

Tiphareth represents the mid-point between the world of everyday reality and the realm of ultimate spiritual transcendence on the journey of mystical growth. It is here that the individual experiences spiritual rebirth. The sphere of Tiphareth is associated with gods of spiritual rebirth and resurrection (Osiris, Mithras and Jesus all belong here mythologically). Tiphareth is symbolised by the Sun as a giver of life and light.

NETZACH

Associated with the planet Venus, Netzach is the sphere of intuition. It represents the arts, creativity and the emotions.

It is also the sphere of love and spiritual passion.

HOD

Associated with the planet Mercury, this sphere represents intellect and rational thinking. In mythological terms, Hod is a lower aspect of the Great Father (Chokmah: Wisdom) and Mercury is the 'messenger' of the higher gods. Hod also symbolises the sense of order that we perceive in the manifested universe.

YESOD

Associated with the Goddess of the Moon, the sphere of Yesod receives impulses and fluxes from the higher realms upon the Tree of Life. Consequently, Yesod abounds in an ocean of astral imagery and is appropriately associated with the element Water. Yesod is also the symbolic centre of the sexual instinct, and on the body of Adam Kadmon this sphere is located over the genitals.

MALKUTH

Associated with the earth, crops, the immediate environment and all living things, as a sphere of consciousness Malkuth represents the beginning of the inner journey. In Roman mythology the entrance to the underworld was through a cave near Naples. Symbolically, Malkuth is the entrance through the earth leading to the underworld – or, in psychological terms, the subconscious mind. Malkuth represents familiar, everyday consciousness. In Greek mythology, the earth sphere of Malkuth is associated with Persephone.

*

In the Western magical tradition, the ten spheres of consciousness on the Kabbalistic Tree of Life can also be combined with the 22 Major Arcana of the Tarot, which then become symbolic pathways linking each of the spheres in turn. We can now consider the symbolism of the Major Arcana as an adjunct to the Kabbalistic Tree of Life.

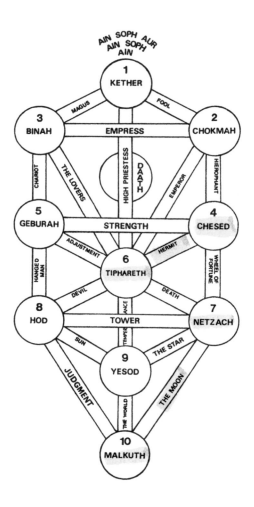

The Major Arcana of the Tarot

In the popular imagination, Tarot cards are associated primarily with divination and gypsy fortune-telling. However, we know that medieval Tarot cards existed in Italy a century before the gypsies arrived there, so the origin of the Tarot remains a genuine mystery.

Some people continue to claim that the Tarot originated in ancient Egypt, a view first put forward by 18th-century French theologian Antoine Court de Gebelin, author of one of the early books on the Tarot, *Le Monde Primitif*. De Gebelin encouraged this theory by claiming that the Tarot was part of an initiatory procedure carried out in the Great Pyramid. However, an examination of the Tarot cards reveals clear references to symbols of chivalry and armoured knights. It is likely, therefore, that even though the imagery in the various Tarot decks is diverse, the Tarot itself is of medieval European origin.

It was the French occultist Eliphas Levi (1810–1875) who first suggested combining the Major Arcana of the Tarot with the Kabbalistic symbol of the Tree of Life. This meant that for the first time Tarot cards could be used not only for divination but as potential pathways into the sacred, mythological spheres of human consciousness.

The 22 cards or Major Arcana of the Tarot – as distinct from the 56 standard cards which are divided into four suits – describe a number of archetypal images. These 'mythic' cards take the form of various male archetypes, including the Magus, the Emperor, the Charioteer and the High Priest, and female counterparts like the High Priestess, the Empress, Justice and the Moon. There are also cards which are symbolically neutral in gender like Death and the Wheel of Fortune.

In the Tarot, the cards of the Major Arcana represent symbolic paths to transcendent reality – a type of spiritual journey through the mazeway of the mind and soul – and, as we have said, in the Western esoteric tradition they have been positioned on the Kabbalistic Tree of Life to produce a composite framework of Western mythic consciousness. However, while the Kabbalah belongs to the Jewish spiritual tradition, the Tarot draws on other spiritual traditions for its imagery. In some Tarot packs, there are Egyptian motifs – the Wheel of Fortune is sometimes shown with the jackal-headed god Hermanubis, and the High Priestess is invariably shown seated between Egyptian-style temple pillars. Figures like the Magus, while medieval in terms of their imagery, are essentially Gnostic in tone – a hint that the medieval Tarot may have been disguising mystical ideas which in the Middle Ages would have been considered heretical. In most Tarot packs the Magician is shown directing spiritual energy from a higher source – the Infinite World of Light – down to the manifested world of form, represented in turn by the symbols of Earth, Water, Fire and Air.

When the 22 Tarot cards of the Major Arcana are mapped as mythic pathways linking the ten different spheres of the Kabbalistic Tree of Life, from the lowest level to the highest, we arrive at a pattern like this: the World (Malkuth-Yesod); Judgment (Malkuth-Hod); the Moon (Malkuth-Netzach); the Sun (Yesod-Hod); the Star (Yesod-Netzach); the Tower (Hod-Netzach); the Devil (Hod-Tiphareth); Death (Netzach-Tiphareth); Temperance (Yesod-Tiphareth); the Hermit (Tiphareth-Chesed); Justice (Tiphareth-Geburah); the Hanged Man (Hod-Geburah); the Wheel of Fortune (Netzach-Chesed); Strength (Geburah-Chesed); the Chariot (Geburah-Binah); the Lovers (Tiphareth-Binah); the Hierophant

(Chesed-Chokmah); the Emperor (Tiphareth-Chokmah); the Empress (Binah-Chokmah); the High Priestess (Tiphareth-Kether); the Magus (Binah-Kether); the Fool (Chokmah-Kether).

We can now consider each of these mythological cards of the Major Arcana in turn.

THE WORLD

The World represents the descent into the underworld of the subconscious mind. In Greek mythology this theme is personified by Persephone and her descent into the land of the dead. Symbolically, death is the other side of life, and Persephone symbolises the wheat grain which grows, dies, and undergoes a perpetual cycle of harvests. Persephone dies to live again: her existence is manifest both in the realm of the living and the dead. In the card of the World she is depicted as androgynous, representing both male and female polarities despite her more obvious femininity.

JUDGMENT

In the same way that Persephone represents both death and life in Greek mythology, Judgment is similarly associated with the theme of rebirth. Here we see figures rising from coffins with their hands in the air. They are gesturing with their arms to form the word *LVX* – 'light' – as they rise in triumph from the grave of ignorance.

THE MOON

The Moon typically mirrors the symbolism of the lunar sphere Yesod, and a lunar crescent dominates the imagery of the card. Two dogs are shown barking at the sky, one of them domesticated and the other untamed. The dog is sacred to the lunar goddess Hecate, who is also associated with Persephone in her deathlike aspect. The Moon describes the ebb and flow of the tides and is symbolic of spiritual evolution. A lobster is shown emerging from the sea to reinforce this effect.

THE SUN

The Sun reflects the light of Tiphareth, which is positioned above it on the Tree of Life. Young naked twins (a boy and a girl) are shown dancing in a magical ring beneath the Sun. They represent both a type of innocence and also the synthesis of opposites – a common theme in the Tarot. They are clearly ruled by the Sun, representing unity, vitality and the path of enlightenment. However, here they are separated from the cosmic mountain by a wall. In an occult sense, the children are still young and inexperienced in their mystical quest; barriers still exist, barring their access to the more sacred regions of the Tree of Life.

THE STAR

The Star is associated with intuition, meditation and the hidden qualities of Nature, represented by Netzach. The beautiful naked White Isis – a lunar deity – kneels by a pool pouring water from flasks held in both hands. One of these flasks is made of gold (equating with the Sun) and the other of silver (equating with the Moon). Reaching up towards a golden star in the sky, the goddess transmits the star's life-energy down to the world below. We learn here that we must each become a pure vessel if we are to attain higher spiritual awareness.

THE TOWER

As a path upon the Tree of Life, the Tower reaches right up to the highest sphere of Kether – that is to say, it embraces the entire universe. A lightning flash strikes its upper turrets, causing it to crumble, and figures are shown falling to their deaths. The Tower serves as a reminder that humility is required on the inner journey, and that the influx of divine energy from the higher realms of the Tree will produce a devastating effect unless our 'magical personality' is well balanced and has a solid foundation. The Tower is ruled by Mars, who ruthlessly destroys ignorance and vain conceptions.

THE DEVIL

Here we are shown a demonic man and woman bound by chains to a pedestal upon which sits a gloating, torch-bearing, goat-headed Devil, representing darkness and bestiality. Upon his brow rests an inverted pentagram, indicating that his spiritual aspirations are directed more towards Earth than towards the transcendental realms of higher consciousness. In this context, the Devil reflects the plight of all unenlightened human beings, with their limited knowledge and understanding. Nevertheless, the light of Tiphareth lies beyond, so all is not lost.

DEATH

Like the Devil, Death indicates humanity's shortcomings and the limited nature of the ego-bound personality. But in the mystical traditions death is also the herald of new life, and beyond the scythe-wielding skeleton figure seen in the foreground of the card we see new light appearing on the horizon. The scythe is associated with Kronos, the ancient

Greek creator-god who transcended time, and on the Tree of Life the path of Death leads into Tiphareth, the sphere of spiritual awakening. So, despite its confronting imagery, the path through Death takes us towards rebirth.

TEMPERANCE

This card represents the line of direct mystical ascent to a state of spiritual illumination. The archangel of Air, Raphael, stands astride a river of light, pouring the waters of Life from a Sun-vessel into a Moon-vessel. This constitutes a 'tempering', or union of opposites – a blending of solar and lunar energies. Raphael has one foot on earth and the other in water and is shown reconciling a white eagle (representing the Moon) and a red lion (representing the Sun). Above him arches a beautiful rainbow symbolising God's covenant with humanity, and new light is dawning over a distant mountain peak.

THE HERMIT

Having reached Tiphareth, we now begin to move towards Kether at the mystical peak of the Tree of Life. The path between Tiphareth and Chesed is ruled by Mercury, who in turn connects with Chokmah and Thoth – the 'Great Father' archetypes of the Kabbalah and the Egyptian mysteries. The Hermit wends his way up the magic mountain but his final goal is firmly in his mind, and the lamp he holds aloft illumines his pathway.

JUSTICE

In Eastern mysticism, Justice would be considered a path of karma – a path where one encounters the consequences of one's actions. Justice demands balance, adjustment and total impartiality. Ruled by the goddess Venus, this path leads to the sphere of her lover Mars, and is appropriately designated by the figure of Venus holding scales and the sword of justice. On this path one begins to discover one's inner self by overcoming the illusory aspects of outer appearances, which are in themselves barriers to true realisation.

THE HANGED MAN

This path, like that of Justice, leads to Geburah, the sphere of action. The Hanged Man swings by his foot, symbolising sacrifice, but because of the way he is positioned he also seems like a reflection in water, the element ascribed to the path. The head of the Hanged Man is all aglow, shining like a beacon, and we see that he is reflecting inspirational light through to lower levels of the Tree of Life. The waters themselves flow from Binah, the Great Mother, and we must open ourselves to their healing energies.

THE WHEEL OF FORTUNE

Appropriately, this card symbolises the forces of fate and destiny. In Kabbalistic magic, words composed of similar letters have related symbolic meanings, and TARO or ROTA – the word inscribed upon the Wheel of Fortune – reads ATOR in reverse. This is a variant spelling of Hathor, the White Goddess, revealing her influence on this path. The path itself leads to Chesed and comes under the jurisdiction of Jupiter.

STRENGTH

This card is positioned horizontally across the Tree of Life and occupies an equivalent position to the Tower, but higher up. Whereas the Tower separates the ego-based personality from the true spiritual self, Strength represents the gulf between individuality and universality. On this card we are shown a woman prising open the jaws of a lion – a clear message for the triumph of spiritual intuition over brute strength. This symbolises complete mastery over any vestiges of the 'animal soul' that remain in our consciousness.

THE CHARIOT

The Chariot represents motion, and this Tarot card provides a direct reference to the so-called *Merkabah* (chariot) tradition in Kabbalistic mysticism which focused on the visionary journey of the soul from one heavenly palace to another. Here the chariot carries the king to the furthest reaches of his realm, while on the opposite side of the Tree, in Chesed, the ruler of the universe views his kingdom from the stationary vantage point of his heavenly throne. On this path the king is a mediator, reminding us that we all need to become a receptor for or vehicle of light. This is indicated by the central symbolism of the card, which shows the king bearing the Holy Grail.

THE LOVERS

On this path the Lovers (or Twins, representing Gemini) stand naked in the innocence of Eden regained, the Holy Guardian Angel towering above them, bestowing grace. Greek mythology records a legend describing the bond between the half-brothers Castor and Polydeuces (Pollux), one mortal and the other immortal. In an act of compassion, Zeus allowed both of them a common destiny, placing them in the sky as the constellation known as Gemini. The path of the Lovers flows upwards from Tiphareth (Harmony) and shows the happy and enduring union of opposites.

THE HIEROPHANT

This path reminds us that the paternal, merciful qualities of the Great Father (Chokmah-Chesed) are enhanced by the love and grace of Venus, who rules this card. We find here an enduring bond of wisdom and mercy. The inspiration of the Spirit is manifest in the Hierophant as an archetypal expression of enlightened intuition. Divine authority owes its inspirational origin to this realm of the Tree of Life.

THE EMPEROR

The Emperor faces towards Chokmah, the 'unmanifested' Great Father of the Trinity, and draws upon Chokmah's spiritual energy as a basis for his authority in governing the universe of Creation below. In the Emperor we find the quality of divine mercy, for although he is capable of aggression in his Geburah aspect, he extends compassion to all his subjects. And the universe itself has come into being through his union with the Empress, or Great Mother.

THE EMPRESS

On this path we enter the realm of pure illumination. The Empress is warm and beneficent. Heavy with child, she is symbolically the Mother of All, since from her womb will flow all the potential images and forms capable of existence in the entire Cosmos. Mythologically she is Hathor and Demeter, and she epitomises Love and Nature on a universal scale. The card depicts her sitting in a field of wheat amid luxuriant trees, with the River of Life flowing forth from her domain. The Empress is the feminine embodiment of the sacred life-energy which emanates from the highest spheres of the Tree of Life.

THE HIGH PRIESTESS

This path, unlike the Empress, reaches to the very peak of Creation – the first sephirah: Kether, the Crown. And the High Priestess herself is unsullied and virginal. She has the potential for motherhood but has not yet brought to fruition the possibility of giving birth – of bringing essence through into form. To this extent she is very much a goddess who belongs in the highest spheres of the Tree of Life. Those who follow her path undergo a dramatic transformation, for they begin to rise above form itself, returning to a pure and undifferentiated state of being.

THE MAGUS

Linked mythologically to Mercury, the cosmic intelligence, the path of the Magus represents the masculine aspect of transcendental spirituality which has not yet found union with its feminine counterpart. This path reflects a type of masculine purity which equates with the virginity of the High Priestess. The Magus stands above Creation in an archetypal sense. He raises one of his hands to Kether so that he may draw its energy down and transmit it to the lower reaches of the Tree of Life.

THE FOOL

The Fool is a symbol for 'he who knows nothing', and this can be interpreted esoterically as well as in an everyday sense. On this path, the magician draws near to the veil of non-existence, 'No-Thing' – that which is unmanifest, or beyond the tangibility of Creation. This is a realm of true Mystery. On the card itself we are shown the Fool about to plunge into the abyss of formlessness, embracing the infinite and sacred transcendence of *Ain Soph Aur*, the Limitless Light.

Alchemy

Alchemy is of interest to us here because it deals with symbols of spiritual transformation. Historically, Western alchemy dates from the beginning of the second century and flourished in Hellenistic Egypt, where there was a high level of proficiency in metalworking skills, especially in relation to silver and copper alloys which resembled gold. Two papyri found in a gravesite in Thebes (the so-called Leiden and Stockholm papyri, which date from around AD 300) include recipes for changing the colour of a metal so that it would resemble gold or silver – a fascinating precursor of the metaphysical concept of the transmutation of base metals into gold.

The word 'alchemy' itself is thought to derive from an Egyptian word, *chem (*or *qem)*, meaning 'black' – a reference to the black alluvial soils bordering the Nile. The fourth-century Egyptian alchemical writer Zosimos of Panopolis (Akhmim) also maintained that a person named Chemes had given rise to the quest for gold and had authored a book of supernaturally inspired instruction called *Chema*, but proof of Chemes's historical existence has not been established. However, we know that in due course the Greek word *chyma*, meaning to fuse or cast metals, established itself in Arabic as *al kimia*, from which the more familiar term 'alchemy' is in turn derived.

As a pagan practice, the study of alchemy thrived in Alexandria in buildings adjacent to the famous Temple of Serapis, but this temple – the Serapeum – together with numerous statues and works of art, was destroyed in 391 on the orders of the Christian archbishop of Alexandria, Theophilus. The persecuted alchemical scholars then withdrew to Athens, and in this way a more comprehensive knowledge of Egyptian alchemy was introduced to Greece. Although pagan traditions were finally suppressed by the emperor Justinian in 529, interest in alchemy was rekindled in the seventh century when Stephanos of Alexandria dedicated his *Nine Lessons in Chemia* to the Byzantine emperor Heraclitus.

The medieval alchemists believed in the unity of the Cosmos and maintained that there was a clear correspondence between the physical and spiritual realms, with comparable laws operating in each domain. As the 16th-century Moravian alchemist Michael Sendivogius wrote in *The New Chemical Light*:

> [The] Sages have been taught of God that this natural world is only an image and material copy of a heavenly and spiritual pattern; that the very existence of this world is based upon the reality of its celestial archetype; and that God has created it in imitation of the spiritual and invisible universe, in order that men might be the better enabled to comprehend His heavenly teaching and the wonders of His absolute and ineffable power and wisdom. Thus the Sage sees heaven reflected in Nature as in a mirror; and he pursues this Art, not for the sake of gold or silver, but for the love of the knowledge which it reveals; he jealously conceals it from the sinner and the scornful, lest the mysteries of heaven should be laid bare to the vulgar gaze.[3]

The alchemists adopted the Hermetic concept that the universe and humanity reflected each other, and in essence this is the core meaning of the idea of the macrocosm and microcosm, and the famous saying, 'As above, so below'. It was assumed by the alchemists that whatever existed in the universe must also, to some degree, be latent or present in every human being. An ancient Hermetic text from Syria makes this point very eloquently:

> What is the adage of the philosophers? Know thyself! This refers to the intellectual and cognitive mirror. And what is this mirror if not the Divine and original Intellect? When a man looks at himself and sees himself in this, he turns away from everything that bears the name of gods or demons, and, by uniting himself with the Holy Spirit, becomes a perfect man. He sees God within himself ...4

In medieval alchemical thought, each individual person consisted of spirit, soul and body, and to this extent contained the very essence of the universe as a whole. The alchemists believed that the Universal Mind was indivisible and united all things in the material universe. The various metals were similarly one in essence, and had sprung from the same seed in the womb of Nature. However, the alchemists did not regard all of the metals as equally mature or 'perfect'. Gold symbolised the highest development in Nature and as an element came to personify human renewal or regeneration. A 'golden' human being was one who was resplendent with spiritual beauty and who had triumphed over temptations and the lurking power of evil. By way of contrast, the most base of all the metals, lead, represented the sinful and unrepentent individual who continued to wallow in sin and was readily overcome by the forces of darkness. As H. Stanley Redgrove has written, 'alchemy was an attempted application of the principles of mysticism to the things of the physical world.'5 Gold was known to resist the action of fire and potential damage from most corrosive liquids, while lead was readily affected by other chemical agents. Meanwhile, the Philosopher's Stone – said to be capable of bringing about a state of alchemical transmutation – was associated by some Christian alchemists with the figure of Jesus himself. Here alchemical transmutation was considered as a type of spiritual redemption and the imagery of base and precious metals provided a metaphor for personal transfiguration.

According to the alchemists, all aspects of matter were a reflection of God, and matter itself consisted of the four elements – Earth, Fire, Air and Water – which in turn proceeded from the *quinta essentia*, or 'quintessence'. Sometimes this symbolic division was represented by a cross within a circle, the four quadrants representing the four elements and the central point the *quinta essentia*. On other occasions the elements were designated by triangles: a triangle pointing upwards representing Fire, because fire 'rises', a triangle pointing downwards representing Water, an upturned triangle with a line through it symbolising Air, and its downward-facing counterpart, Earth. The alchemists also associated certain metals with the astrological 'planets': gold for the Sun, silver for the Moon, quicksilver for Mercury, copper for Venus, iron for Mars, tin for Jupiter and lead for Saturn. However, they believed that the process of transmutation from a base metal into silver or gold was not possible without the metal first being reduced to its *materia prima*, or 'fundamental substance'. This was analagous to reducing each metal initially to a state of 'soul' or 'essence'.

The soul, in its original state of pure receptivity, was regarded by the alchemists as fundamentally one with the *materia prima* of the whole world. The idea of the *materia prima* referred to the potential of 'soul' to take a material form. At this level one could consider a metal to be latent, or 'unrealised'.

The alchemists themselves described a metal in this condition as 'uncongealed' – that is, free of specific qualities. On the other hand, specific metals were normally rigid, restricted or 'coagulated'. Alchemical transformation therefore involved a shift from the initial coagulation through such processes as burning, dissolving and purification, in order to produce a new outcome – a quite different reformulation of the original substance.

On one level, alchemy was a physical attempt to produce gold from base metals, and some practitioners – precursors of modern laboratory scientists – understood it on this level. However, when we realise that alchemy also symbolised the potential for human transformation, we can see that it also described an essentially spiritual process. Just as the alchemists believed that amorphous *materia* could be burned, dissolved, purified and then 'coagulated' into the form of a perfect metal like gold – a literal symbol of wholeness – this process could also be applied to the mystical quest for oneness with God. For the spiritual alchemists, the soul could be born again and find its true home in the realm of Spirit. As Titus Burckhardt has written: 'We are all like waves within the same sea ... The highest meaning of alchemy is the knowledge that all is contained in all, and its *magisterium* is none other than the realisation of this truth on the plane of the soul.'[6]

Wicca and Goddess spirituality

One of the most interesting magical paths today focuses on what is sometimes referred to as the archetypal 'Feminine' – the Universal Goddess. It is hardly surprising that feminine spirituality should have come to the fore in recent times, with the international feminist movement having helped to rectify an obvious male-oriented imbalance in society.

Reverence for the Feminine takes many different forms. It

may be expressed through the sacred metaphor of Gaia, the embodiment of the living planet and of global awareness, or it may derive from the feminist perception that a largely male-dominated society should learn to acquire the 'feminine' gifts of nurturing and intuition. And it is mirrored, too, in the contemporary revival of interest in the esoteric Wiccan and neopagan traditions which honour the Universal Goddess through different ceremonial expressions.

Modern witchcraft is often referred to as Wicca, from the Old English words *wicca* (masculine) and *wicce* (feminine), meaning 'a practitioner of witchcraft'. The word *wiccan*, meaning 'witches', occurs in the Laws of King Alfred (circa 890), and the verb *wiccian* – 'to bewitch' – was also used in this context. Some witches believe the words connote a wise person, hence Wicca is sometimes known as the 'Craft of the Wise'.

Witchcraft is in essence a Nature-based religion with the Great Goddess as its principal deity. She can take many forms: the Great Mother or Mother Nature, or, more specifically, Artemis, Astarte, Athene, Demeter, Diana, Aphrodite, Hathor, Isis, Persephone and many others. The High Priestess of the coven incarnates the spirit of the Goddess in a ceremonial context when the High Priest 'draws down the Moon' into her body. In witchcraft, the High Priestess is the receptacle of wisdom and intuition and is symbolised by the cup, while her consort, the High Priest, is represented by a short sword or dagger. Many witchcraft rituals feature the act of uniting dagger and cup as a symbol of sexual union, and there is also a comparable relationship in Celtic mythology between the sacred oak tree and Mother Earth. Accordingly the High Priest is sometimes known as the Oak King – a reference to the Oak of the Celts – and at other times as Cernunnos, 'The Horned One'. In witchcraft the Horned God personifies fertility, and in ancient Greece the Great God Pan, the goat-footed god, was a symbol of Nature and the universal life-force. There is no connection between the Horned God of witchcraft and the Christian horned Devil, although, ever since the witchcraft persecutions of the Middle Ages, this has been a common error.

Wiccan covens vary in size, but traditionally the membership number is thirteen, consisting of six men, six women and the High Priestess. When the group exceeds this number, some members leave to form a new coven. Wiccans take special magical names which they use in a ritual context, and they meet for their ceremonies at specific times of the year. These meetings, or sabbats, are related to the cycles of Nature and the traditional times for harvesting crops.

The four major sabbats are Candlemas (2 February), known by the Celts as *Imbolc* (celebrated on 1 August in the southern hemisphere); May Eve (30 April), or *Beltane* (celebrated on 31 October in the southern hemisphere); Lammas (1 August), or *Lughnassadh* (celebrated on 2 February in the southern hemisphere); Halloween (31 October), or *Samhain* (celebrated on 30 April in the southern hemisphere). In addition, there are four minor sabbats – the two solstices at midsummer and midwinter, and the two equinoxes in spring and autumn.

In pre-Christian times, *Imbolc* was traditionally identified with the first signs of spring; *Beltane* was a fertility celebration when the sacred oak was burned, mistletoe cut, and sacrifices made to the gods; *Lughnassadh*, which was related to autumn and the harvesting of crops, celebrated both the gathering in of produce and the continuing fertility of the earth; and *Samhain* represented the transition from autumn to winter and was associated with bonfires to keep away the chilly winter winds. *Samhain* was also a time when the spirits of the dead could return to Earth to be once again with their loved ones.

Contemporary witches still meet in their covens to celebrate these Celtic rites (in the southern hemisphere, as detailed above, most Wiccan practitioners adjust the sabbats to equate with the appropriate season). Sabbats are a time for fellowship, ceremony and initiation, and after the rituals have been performed there is feasting, drinking and merriment.

Wiccan ceremonies take place in a magic circle which can either be inscribed on the floor of a special room set aside as the 'temple', or marked on the earth at a designated meeting place – for example, in a grove of trees or on the top of a sacred hill. The earth is swept with a ritual broomstick for purification and the four elements are ascribed to the four directions: Earth in the north, Air in the east, Fire in the south and Water in the west. The altar is traditionally placed in the north. Beings known as the 'Lords of the Watchtowers' govern the four quarters and are invoked in rituals for blessings and protection.

Within the circle and present on the altar are the Wiccans' *Book of Shadows* (a personal book of rituals and invocations), a bowl of water, a dish of salt, candles, a symbolic scourge (representing will and determination), a bell, a cord to bind candidates in initiation, and consecrated symbols of the elements: a pentacle or disc (Earth/feminine); a cup (Water/feminine); a censer or container in which incense is burned (Fire/masculine); and a wand (Air/masculine). The High Priestess has her own *athame*, or ritual dagger, and the sword of the High Priest rests on the ground before the altar.

Contemporary Wicca recognises three initiations. The first confers witch-status upon the neophyte, the second promotes a first-degree witch to the position of High

Priestess or High Priest, and the third celebrates the bonding of the High Priestess and High Priest in the Great Rite: either real or symbolic sexual union.[7]

There is also an emphasis in Wicca on the threefold aspect of the Great Goddess in her role as maid (youth, enchantment), mother (maturity, fulfilment) and crone (old age, wisdom). These symbolic personifications of the phases of womanhood are represented, for example, by the Celtic triad Brigit (Danu) Morrigan, the Greek goddess in her three aspects Persephone–Demeter–Hecate, or by the three Furies, Alecto (goddess of beginnings), Tisiphone (goddess of continuation) and Megaera (goddess of death and rebirth). This threefold aspect is particularly emphasised by feminist Wicca groups in their development of 'women's mysteries'. As American neopagan Z. Budapest writes in her *Holy Book of Women's Mysteries*, 'Images of the Mother Goddess, female principle of the universe and source of all life, abound ... [for she is] the goddess of ten thousand names.'[8]

On a practical level, Wiccan ceremonies can involve spells of enchantment, invocations for healing and initiations which lead a coven member from one grade of advancement to the next. Witches also conduct their own type of weddings, known as 'handfastings', which bind Wiccans for a specified time ranging from a year and a day to 'eternity', and also 'wiccanings', the pagan counterpart of christenings. A coven functions rather like a family, with the High Priestess and High Priest taking a caring, parental role over the group members.

One of the areas where Wicca differs from more organised religions is in its conviction that the divine principle can be found, potentially, within every living person. A formal structure or belief system is not required. Margot Adler, granddaughter of the famous psychologist Alfred Adler and the acclaimed author of *Drawing Down the Moon*, a detailed study of American neopaganism, says, 'The fundamental thing about the magical and pagan religions is that ultimately they say that within yourself you are the god, you are the goddess – you can actualise within yourself and create whatever you need on this earth and beyond.'[9]

Miriam Simos, another key figure in the Wiccan movement, regards her magical craft as the ability to transform consciousness at will and believes the female practitioner has a special and privileged role. As a representative of the Goddess, the female Wiccan is, metaphorically, a giver of life. According to Simos (otherwise known as Starhawk):

'The images of the Goddess as birth-giver, weaver, earth and growing plant, wind and ocean, flame, web, moon and milk, all speak to me of connectedness, sustenance, healing, creating ... My model of power says that the world itself is sacred and the Goddess is simply our name for the living organism of which we're all a part.'[10]

Shamanism

There is a widespread recognition today that indigenous peoples live their lives more closely and qualitatively attuned to the cycles of Nature than those of us who live in urban settings. And it is the native mythology of the earth and sky, of the Cosmos and the founding ancestors, associated in turn with a more innate understanding of the archetypal forces which shape our world, that endears many people to the indigenous peoples who remain scattered across the surface of the planet. Rightly or wrongly, and perhaps at times romantically, a perception has arisen of an ancient native wisdom, an authentic way of living, which we have lost and which we could, perhaps, regain. A sense of this is captured in the Navajo song:

> *The thoughts of earth are my thoughts*
> *The voice of earth is my voice*
> *All that belongs to the earth belongs to me*
> *All that surrounds the earth surrounds me*
> *It is lovely indeed; it is lovely indeed.*

This type of holistic consciousness is also found in the account of the Oglala Sioux medicine man, Black Elk, who stood on the summit of Harney Peak in the Black Hills of South Dakota and experienced a vision of the universe uplifted by a profound sense of harmony and balance:

> I was standing on the highest mountain of them all, and round about me was the whole hoop of the world and while I stood there I saw more than I can tell and I understood more than I saw, for I was seeing in a sacred manner the shapes of things in the spirit, and the shape of all shapes as they must live together like one being. And I saw that the sacred hoop of my people was one of many hoops that made one circle, wide as daylight and as starlight, and in the centre grew one mighty flowering tree to shelter all the children of one mother and one father. And I saw that it was holy.[11]

Similarly, Galarrwuy Yunupingu, a Yolngu Aboriginal from the Yirrkala community in north-east Arnhem Land, has expressed his deep love of the earth:

> The land is my backbone ... I only stand straight, happy,

proud and not ashamed about my colour because I still have land. I can paint, dance, create and sing as my ancestors did before me. I think of land as the history of my nation. It tells of how we came into being and what system we live ... My land is mine only because I came in spirit from that land and so did my ancestors of the same land ... My land is my foundation.[12]

It is this rediscovery of the bond that native peoples feel with the sacred earth that has led many people to explore indigenous belief systems and the most ancient spiritual tradition of all: shamanism. Shamanism is not only the earliest but is also the most widespread spiritual tradition in human culture, extending back to the Palaeolithic era. Remnants of it are still found as far afield as Siberia, the United States, Mexico, Central and South America, Japan, Tibet, Indonesia, Nepal and Aboriginal Australia.

From earliest times, shamans have mimicked birds and animals in their magical rituals and have revered sacred plants. They have developed what we would now call a 'holistic' relationship with the Cosmos.

Shamanism, though, is more than just imitative magic. It can be regarded as an animistic approach to Nature and the Cosmos, which utilises visionary states of consciousness as a means of contacting the denizens of the spirit world. The shaman – who can be a man or a woman, depending on cultural determinants – is essentially a magical practitioner who, through an act of will, can enter into a state of trance and who then journeys to the land of the gods or perhaps, closer to home, divines by visionary means the causes of sickness and malaise.

Underlying all forms of shamanism is the notion that the

universe is alive with gods and spirits. The shaman's role is to divine the presence of harmful or malicious spirits which are causing individual illness or which are 'cursing' members of the tribal group. The healer-shaman is thus an intermediary between the natural and metaphysical worlds, meeting the spirits on their own territory.

A classic example of shamanic journeying is found in an account of a Shaman in Siberia. The Nanay people of the Tungus region greatly respect the capacity of the shaman to journey between the worlds. In a state of trance, the shaman descends to the 'lower world' and meets magical animals who act as spirit guides. During his initiatory visionary journey, the Nanay shaman is suckled by a goddess known as the Mistress of the Water and then, with his animal guides, is shown a community of spirits responsible for causing sickness in the world. Later the shaman 'flies' in his spirit-body to the top of an enormous tree which then speaks to him: 'I am the tree that makes all people capable of living.' The tree spirit then provides the shaman with a branch with three shoots. These, he is told, are to be used in the construction of three special drums: one for performing shamanic rituals over women in childbirth, the second for treating the sick, and the third for aiding those who are dying.

In Siberia the drum has always had a special role, because it is on the rhythmic drumbeat that the shaman 'rides' into a state of ecstasy. And the idea of shamanism as a 'journey' into the metaphysical world is a feature not only of Nanay cosmology but of shamanic cultures generally. It therefore comes as no surprise that among the Jivaro of eastern Ecuador, for example, the normal everyday world is considered to be false or a 'lie', while the truth about the real nature of things is to be found only by entering the supernatural world.[13] Undertaking this vision quest is the role of the shaman.

BECOMING A SHAMAN

Shamanism is a magical vocation. Some shamans adopt their role in society as part of an ancestral lineage, while others are called to the path through dreams or spirit-visions. The Chukchee of Siberia say that future shamans have a certain look in their eyes which indicates that they can see beyond the domain of everyday reality to the realm of spirit. And perhaps because this visionary capacity is restricted to just a few, shamans have often found themselves on the edge of society. Often introverted and sometimes suffering from disease or misfortune themselves, potential shamans function in parallel mental universes and, as a result, some psychiatrists have compared them to schizophrenics. There is, however, a crucial difference between shamans and schizophrenics. Schizophrenics move in and out of different mental states continually and without control, thus dwelling in a world of experiential chaos, while shamans have to learn to integrate their visionary capacities and subject them to the individual will. For this reason, the noted scholar of comparative religion, Mircea Eliade, has defined the shaman or medicine man as one 'who has succeeded in curing himself'. With this self-mastery comes the ability to undertake spirit-journeys, to drive away evil spirits and to cure the sick.

Often during the initiatory process of becoming a shaman there are special revelations. Isaac Tens, a North American Gitksan Indian, began falling into trance states when he was 30 and frequently experienced terrifying visions. On one occasion, animal spirits and snake-like trees seemed to be chasing him and an owl tried to attack him and lift him up. Later, on a hunting trip, Tens again saw an owl and shot it. When he went to collect the body, however, he was unable to locate it. He fell into a trance, his body began to 'boil' and 'quiver' and he found he was singing spontaneously. 'A chant was coming out of me without my being able to do anything to stop it,' he explained. 'Many things appeared to me presently: huge birds and other animals. They were calling me. I saw a *meskyawawderh* [a kind of bird] and a *mesqag-weeuk* [a bullhead fish]. These were visible only to me, not to the others in my house.'[14]

The Paviotso shaman Dick Mahwee had his first shamanic visions while dreaming in a cave. Aged around 50, Mahwee was in a state of 'conscious sleep' when he had a mystical encounter with a tall, thin Indian holding an eagle tail-feather. The Indian instructed him in ways of curing sickness, and as a consequence Mahwee now knows that he must enter a trance state if he is to perform shamanic healing:

I smoke before I go into the trance. While I am in the trance no-one makes any noise. I go out to see what will happen to the patient. When I see a whirlwind I know that it causes the sickness. If I see the patient walking on grass and flowers it means that he will get well; he will soon be up and walking. When I see the patient among fresh flowers and he picks them it means that he will recover. If the flowers are withered or look as if frost had killed them, I know that the patient will die. Sometimes in a trance I see the patient walking on the ground. If he leaves footprints I know that he will live, but if there are no tracks, I cannot cure him.[15]

REGALIA AND RITUALS

As noted earlier, the shaman has been traditionally perceived as a master of ecstasy; the shaman's role has always been to fly in the spirit-vision to where the gods were, for it was here that the revelations were received. And since the shaman was able to travel from one dimension of perceptual reality to another, it was understandable that his rituals and costume would embody all that was sacred or mythically relevant within the given culture.

Sometimes shamans would decorate their clothing with motifs relating to their magical animal allies, or with important symbols from their mythology. Traditional Japanese shamans, for example, wore caps of eagle and owl feathers and their cloaks were adorned with stuffed snakes. Siberian Yakut shamans wore kaftans embellished with a solar disc – thought to be the opening through the earth leading to the Underworld – while Goldi shamans wore coats depicting the Cosmic Tree and magical animals like bears and leopards. Buryats wore costumes laden with iron implements, symbolising the iron bones of immortality, and also employed motifs representing the bears, serpents and lizards that they had befriended as their helper spirits.

Shamans, as we have already noted, imitate birds and animals in their dances. Yakuts could imitate the lapwing, falcon, eagle and cuckoo, while Kirghiz shamans learned not only bird songs but also how to imitate the sounds of their wings in flight. Zuni Pueblo Indians still summon their Beast Gods in ceremonies involving dancing, rattling and drumming. Wearing ritual masks, they work themselves into a state of frenzy wherein they feel they are becoming the animals themselves through an act of ritual identification. According to anthropologist Dr Michael Harner, who has observed them, the Zuni dancers are doing much more than simply impersonating animal forms. Transported into an altered state of consciousness by the dancing, drumming, rattling and whirr of bull-roarers, the shaman 'becomes for the time being the actual embodiment of the spirit which is believed to reside in the mask'.[16]

As one can see from accounts like this, the drum plays a vital role in shamanic practice: it is literally the vehicle that carries the shaman into the magical world. The rhythmic sound of the drumbeat acts as a focusing device for the shaman, enabling him to enter the trance state in a controlled way. Some shamans also embellish their drums in ways that are symbolically significant. Lapp shamans decorate their drums with motifs like the Cosmic Tree, the Sun, the moon, or a rainbow, while traditional Evenks fashioned their drum rims from sacred larch.

HELPER SPIRITS

In divining the origins of sickness, some healer-shamans call on magical helper spirits, or 'allies'. There are many different terms for these entities – they are variously known as 'guardian spirits', 'dream healers' or 'power animals' – but it is generally agreed by scholars of comparative religion that healer-shamans need spirit guides of one form or another in their divinatory practices. As Dr Michael Harner has observed, 'A shaman may be defined as a man or woman who is in direct contact with the spirit world through a trance state and has one or more spirits at his command to carry out his bidding for good or evil.'[17]

These allies appear to the shaman in dreams and visions and in some circumstances can be inherited from other shamans or family elders. Allies can be summoned into action through songs and dances and often require ritualistic offerings. Some shamans have even claimed to be married to their spirit guides!

The divinatory functions of helper spirits are diverse. They might be sent by the shaman into the patient's body in order to detect the cause of sickness, or they might be despatched in order to locate missing objects. And, as we have seen, healer spirits may also accompany the shaman on the visionary journey to the magical world.

The Yurok Indians of north-western California still practise shamanic healing using spirit guides. Yurok healer Tela Lake describes the shaman as 'a holistic healer who uses the physical and spiritual forces of Nature to effect a cure'.[18] She believes that the soul is the very essence of a human being and that the body, mind and soul are held together by a force-field of power or spirit. It is this energy field that can be treated by the shaman through spirit divination.

Patients abstain from drugs, sex and alcohol for four days prior to a healing ceremony with Tela Lake: they are then considered 'clean'. After the patient arrives, Tela goes outside to consult with her familiar spirits and then accepts or rejects the patient for the healing ceremony (refusal usually arising only when the patient contravenes the spiritual laws of the Yurok in some way). Immediately before the actual ceremony, all participants are required to bathe, and various plants and herbal medicines are used to purify the patient.

As the ceremony begins, the shaman sits in front of her patient, facing east, and invokes her spirits through song and prayer. According to Tela, the spirits assist her in identifying the cause of the patient's problems. She says that some spirits can fly backwards in time to seek the origins of disease, while other 'interpreter' spirits can divine information received magically in different languages. Included among Tela's helper spirits are a woodpecker (able to remove pain from the patient's body) and a hummingbird (able to suck out poison). She also summons bear and wolf 'allies' to fight off sickness, and a spirit-fish to eat away at illness, as the need arises.[19]

The Shoshoni medicine man Tudy Roberts told Professor Ake Hultkrantz that he had spirit helpers of both animal and human appearance after performing a Sun Dance and then falling asleep in the foothills of Fort Washakie, he had contact with three humanoid spirit beings. These spirits looked like Indians but wore feathers in their hats and had 'very clean clothes'. Roberts learned that they were lightning spirits and that they would help him in his healing practices. The spirits showed him how to perform shamanic divination using an eagle tail and an eagle wing, and he subsequently gained the power to treat colds, measles and paralysis. However, Roberts never sought to cure anybody unless he received instructions from his helper spirits in shamanic dream-visions.[20]

Bringing it all together

As we can see, the sources of the Western magical tradition are very diverse and extend far back into history – back to the very earliest expressions of human spiritual awareness. And yet, while the symbolism of these different mystical perspectives can at times be complex, I believe that we can draw practical lessons from each of these magical traditions. Here are some of the core spiritual truths from each of these traditions:

The Kabbalah Everything in the material world proceeds from a sacred and infinite source which is beyond form.

The Major Arcana of the Tarot We can follow different paths home to the true origin of our being, but they all lead finally to the infinite realm of Spirit.

Alchemy As above, so below. The Cosmos is reflected on Earth. As we grow towards Spirit, each of us must pass through different stages of personal transformation.

Wicca and Goddess spirituality We owe our existence to the Great Mother. All things born in this world have come forth from the womb of the Universal Goddess.

Shamanism Everything in the Universe is alive – everything is Spirit.

CHAPTER TWO

First steps on the visionary path

O ne of the main ideas in magic is that each of us can become what we aspire to be, that basically the only barriers limiting our visionary potential are those which we impose upon ourselves through the restraints of our imagination. After all, what we believe about ourselves defines the territory for our personal development. We can fence ourselves in with negative or restrictive belief systems and concepts, or we can seek options in our lives which are liberating, transforming and empowering. The second of these two options is what positive magic is all about.

Although we have all heard tales of people casting magic spells on hapless victims or seeking to bewitch their adversaries with occult rites and incantations, authentic magical empowerment is not about using magical techniques to dominate others or to get ahead at someone else's expense.

Ultimately, magical attainment has more to do with tapping into our own sacred potential, with becoming a vehicle for positive and creative outcomes, and with manifesting in our lives a sense of meaning and purpose which reflects our core sense of inner authenticity.

Some people equate magic with illusionism and disguises – even with trickery and deception. But authentic magic – *real* magic – is about recognising who we are, establishing what we want from life and what we can offer others, and then envisioning outcomes which will provide our life with meaning and purpose. Once we can imagine ourselves on a transformative path, a path which reflects our true nature and purpose, our lives will then begin to mirror these magical realities. With effort, what we envision for our lives will ultimately become true for us in our everyday experience.

Recognising who we are

Most of us in modern Western society are very effectively programmed by prevailing cultural norms. We learn early on that our survival in everyday life depends primarily upon establishing our ego or persona – the self we present to the world – and playing it for all it is worth in an increasingly competitive and often unfriendly world which respects strength above weakness. We are encouraged to speak up for ourselves, and it is brought home to us at an early age that society doesn't owe us a living. Most of us are also taught by our parents or peers that there is virtue in positive effort, and that good things come to those who work hard for them. As we grow up we also learn that society seems to reward those who assert their needs and project their personal image most effectively onto others, whether at home, at school or at work. Our daily focus, more often than not, becomes one of ever-expanding ego-fulfilment, with a strong emphasis on individual careers and material gain.

Many of us become increasingly competitive – and often more aggressive – as we seek to get further ahead of our fellow travellers, and if we are inclined by nature to be devious or ruthless we may also develop strategies that ensure our advancement is at the expense of others. At the same time, we probably also develop an increasing pride in our accumulated material possessions, which then become a form of tangible proof that all our efforts have been worthwhile.

In the midst of all this, we must sooner or later come to recognise *who we really are and what we are doing in our life.* Do we define ourselves mostly in terms of our possessions, our material prosperity, or by our level of seniority in the workplace? If we do, that's fine – magic can work very effectively on this level, as we will see. Nevertheless, magic of the material sphere is sometimes referred to as 'basic magic' or 'low magic' because making magic on this level is based solely on physical rather than on spiritual or holistic outcomes. Magic performed on this level does not involve any sense of spiritual commitment, nor does it usually relate to the personal growth of the individual. It is simply about manifesting physical things which we are seeking in our everyday life.

However, as I hope to show in this book, magic is not only about material gain or ego gratification. Many people who are attracted to the visionary path in magic are seeking a different sense of self, one which has more to do with self-exploration or self-realisation, and they are embarking on an inner journey where the rewards are more spiritual than material. Here our sense of recognising who we are demands of us that we explore our true inner nature, not just our external persona and its role in the physical world, and also that we do this in a way which will provide us with a sense of meaning and purpose in relation to the broader scheme of things. This is a perspective which is potentially so far-reaching that it will eventually link us with all other living creatures in our immediate environment, and finally with the Universe as a whole.

When we add this depth of perception to our daily lives, our social and business activities take on an altogether different character. It is not then so much a matter of endlessly competing against others in order to feel personally fulfilled but, rather, an ever-developing process of working in tandem with our fellow travellers. This involves acknowledging personal strengths and weaknesses in different individuals while recognising that all aspects of human endeavour are eventually part of a much broader spectrum of awareness and activity, a spectrum which finally transcends the efforts of any particular individual. From this broader viewpoint we can finally recognise a shared sense of purpose for all human beings on the planet.

Magic practised for spiritual development is sometimes known as 'high magic', because its aspirations are towards that which resonates at a higher level on the scale of spiritual attainment. This form of magic is higher not because it is *better*, but because ultimately it is *truer*. And it is truer because, from a magical perspective, it is closer to the universal source of life.

Magical aspirations

One of the hardest things for us to resolve is establishing what we truly want from life. When we are establishing our personal priorities, what things come first to mind? Are we seeking financial prosperity and security? Are we focusing primarily on our personal relationships with others? Are we mostly preoccupied with receiving respect and acknowledgment from our family, friends and peers, or in attaining an even broader scale of recognition involving national or international fame? These may be some of the things which come to mind as we assess our most deeply felt priorities in life. And once again, it isn't a matter of judging whether any of these aspirations is more worthy than some of the others. Making magic on any level involves recognising who we are and what we seek. We can only manifest our goals on the basis of our own personal vision for ourselves. How broad this vision will be is entirely up to us.

Because one of the principal magical techniques involves making affirmations in combination with creative visualisation, it may be useful at this stage to start your own magical diary and to list on the first page your mostly deeply felt magical aspirations. What are the things you most want to acquire or have access to (through physical-level magic)? What states of wellbeing are you seeking in your life, either with regard to yourself or in your relationships with others (through emotional-level magic)? What are your holistic goals which define your relationships, not only with your immediate friends and family but also with your environment, with the world, and with the Universe at large (through spiritual-level magic)? We should reflect once again on the fact that magic has no boundaries, for we are only constrained by the limits of our imagination. As the well-known researcher of human potentials Dr John Lilly once put it: 'In the province of the mind, what is believed to be true is true, or becomes true, within certain limits to be found experientially and experimentally. These limits are further beliefs to be transcended. In the province of the mind, there are no limits.'[1]

As we have seen, the essential task of practical magic is to envision outcomes and to make them come true in our everyday lives. And these outcomes can be on any level we choose to focus on. Identifying specific tasks and developing relationships which will provide our personal lives with meaning and purpose is very much a matter of individual choice. The magic we pursue will obviously reflect our goals and ideals. All of which brings us now to consider the hard part of magic – putting it into practice in our everyday lives.

I think most practitioners and devotees of the various paths in magic would agree that the following skills are crucial to our personal growth as we seek to develop our magical and spiritual awareness: creative visualisation, rhythmic breathing and colour visualisation, positive affirmations, magical imaging.

In this book we will draw on all of the major magical and metaphysical traditions presented in the previous chapter, for these collectively represent a proven wisdom path for the modern world. Some of the techniques and magical skills will come from the Kabbalah, Wicca and the Tarot, while the metaphors and processes of spiritual transformation from alchemy and shamanism will also be explored. Many of these techniques and approaches will be described in more detail in subsequent chapters of this book, but for the moment it will be useful if we focus now on some of the basic skills required on the magical path.

*

Creative visualisation

Creative visualisation is sometimes called 'active meditation', or 'seeing with the mind's eye'. Many familiar forms of Eastern meditation involve eliminating imagery from consciousness altogether, thereby removing the distractions provided by the visual and verbal chatter of the mind. However, although creative visualisation can be regarded as a form of meditation, it has a somewhat different emphasis to Eastern meditation. Rather than negating visual imagery, it involves summoning into our sphere of perception specific images which will be helpful in providing insights and solutions that relate directly to personal issues in our life.

Creative visualisation teaches us to use the powers of our imagination to find out more about ourselves, to solve problems we may be experiencing, and also to change those entrenched attitudes and beliefs that we continue to hold on to as the very cornerstones of our existence. But a central point – and this relates specifically to all forms of visionary magic – is that by using the techniques of creative visualisation we can make something happen in our lives through an act of *willed intention*. We can utilise our imagination in order to anticipate change and to envision different outcomes. This realisation invariably brings with it a certain momentum – a sense of real excitement at the promise of what is yet to unfold – and this allows us to expand our spectrum of awareness still further.

When we use the techniques of creative visualisation for a magical purpose we learn to draw on the potentials of our mind in a more complete way than we usually have in the past. In doing this, we are drawing not only on our memories of the physical world and our place in it, but we are also delving into the subconscious and spiritual levels of our mind. This may involve engaging with symbols or images which arise spontaneously, or which have appeared to us in dreams or in states of reverie. It may also involve those powerful images which Swiss psychoanalyst Carl Jung called 'archetypes' – personifications of universal sacred energies which in all cultures and traditions have inspired religions, mythologies and a rich variety of artistic expressions.

It is important to emphasise, though, that we ought to interpret specific images for ourselves and learn to receive the lessons which the mind and spirit present to us in an open and receptive manner. Although it is always wise for us to listen to the advice of our friends and teachers, eventually each one of us will have to learn to become the sole authority on our own process of personal growth and increased magical awareness. In this regard, we should anticipate that the images which arise through our exploration of creative visualisation will engage us in a direct and personal way. No interpretations of visionary imagery are ever fixed or immutable; the particular meanings of individual images vary greatly from person to person and it is up to us to heed the lessons provided by these images.

An important principle of creative visualisation is to engage with the images which arise into consciousness *as if they were real*. Creative visualisation means evoking images into consciousness in such a way that they have a three-dimensional presence and are both convincing and alive within our spectrum of awareness. To do this effectively we will be drawing on images and impressions from our memories, from our senses, from our emotions and from the deepest and most spiritual regions of our minds.

When we practise creative visualisation as part of our magical orientation, it is a good idea to focus on the positive rather than the negative, and also to visualise what we actually want rather than what we don't want. Although this may seem like stating the obvious it is nevertheless one of the central principles of positive everyday magic.

GETTING STARTED – WITH RELAXATION

Most people find that the best way to begin practising creative visualisation is to learn first of all how to relax. There are many ways of doing this and you will have to find a way that works for you. Relaxation provides us with a sense of openness and inner stillness that then allows the magic to happen.

Here is one approach to relaxation that I have found helpful as a prelude to creative visualisation. Sit comfortably on the floor or in a chair, loosen any items of clothing that are likely to provide distraction or discomfort, and then begin progressively to relax different parts of your body. You might like to begin by visualising that your feet are becoming increasingly limp and relaxed, and then that your ankles and your calves have also relaxed in turn. Imagine now that your legs are completely relaxed and then that a soothing feeling of relaxation has entered your abdomen and is working its way into your upper body. Now your chest is becoming completely relaxed and you are breathing deeply and without restriction. Finally you relax your arms and allow the focus of your attention to remain solely in your head. And now your focus is on awareness itself, for from this point onwards your emphasis will be on summoning into your field of vision those images which will help you engage with the task at hand.

VISUALISING THE SENSES

A good way to start practising creative visualisation is to focus on each of your senses in turn – smell, touch, taste, sight and hearing. Begin by imagining those *smells* which appeal to you and also those that repel you, and bring these as fully as you can into your conscious awareness. Experience the intoxicating scent of a beautiful rose or the distinctive smell of a freshly peeled mandarin – or any other aroma you find enticing. Then recall the decidedly unpleasant smell of the garbage or a carton of rancid milk.

Now you might like to concentrate on your sense of *touch*. Imagine in your mind's eye that you are running your fingers across someone else's skin. You feel the softness and perhaps also the wrinkles, the little bumps and grooves – the textures which make the surface of the skin so distinctive. Perhaps you can then concentrate on what it is like to feel smooth wood, or rough sandpaper, or the texture of hair?

Next you should focus your awareness on your sense of *taste*. Recall that delicious cup of tea or coffee that you had at breakfast, or the distinctive taste of that luscious mango or peach that you really enjoyed. Now switch your attention to *sight*. Recall the particular colours of objects in your immediate environment – perhaps the colours of the different flowers, grasses and trees in your garden. What colour is the sky overhead? Watch as the power of your imagination allows each object in turn to take its focal place within your field of vision.

Finally, turn your attention to your sense of *hearing*. Listen to the distinctive song of a bird outside in the garden, concentrate on the qualities of a particular person's voice ... what is that makes these sounds so distinctive? Do any of these sounds evoke a particular emotional resonance, or are any of them associated with a particular memory?

As you gradually become attuned to summoning specific images and sensory impressions into your field of awareness you can in turn focus on other ways of enhancing how real they become for you. One way of doing this is by exploring rhythmic breathing in conjunction with colour visualisation.

Rhythmic breathing and colour visualisation

Breath represents vitality and epitomises life itself. By associating visual images with your pattern of breathing you literally bring these images to life and make them real in your perceptual world.

Once you have practised relaxation and have gained a degree of proficiency in visualising the different senses, you can begin to introduce rhythmic breathing as an additional dimension of creative visualisation.

We all recognise instinctively that the way we breathe is important in helping us to relax our body and release any emotional blocks or anxieties that are inhibiting our flow of awareness. As part of developing our skills with breathing we should also learn to focus on the nature of breathing itself by listening closely to its repetitive patterns, engaging with the rhythm of our pulse and heartbeat, and becoming aware of the passage of air as we breathe slowly in and out through our nostrils. We can even visualise our breath, seeing it in our mind's eye as it streams into the body and then flows free again.

For example, some people find it useful to visualise the breath as a stream of pure white light, entering through the crown of the head and then forming a vortex as it passes down through the body. As you do this you can imagine each intake of breath bringing new life and vitality to every cell in your body, just as you can visualise each corresponding exhalation removing anxieties or other negative emotions.

Soon you will come to associate your pattern of breathing with enhancing your inner vitality, building your strength and helping to focus your sense of personal resolve. Visualising your breathing patterns in this way also increases your sense of personal integrity and wholeness.

One of the breathing patterns I have found most useful is the so-called 'four-four' cycle. Here you breathe in to a silent count of four, hold to a count of four, release your breath to a count of four, and then once again hold to a count of four. And so the cycle continues. This pattern of breathing has both a relaxing and an energising effect and is ideal as an adjunct to magical visualisation.

COLOUR BREATHING

Now we may like to add an additional element to our breathing – by visualising specific colours energising each breath. From a holistic perspective, colour breathing is an excellent way of enhancing our sense of vitality and, as we will see later, visualising specific colours in association with the breath is also an important skill in the practice of visionary magic.

Before we look into the symbolic and traditional healing qualities of the various colours, it is important to know something about the Tattvas. These are the five Hindu elements, and for over a hundred years they have been incorporated within the Western magical tradition for purposes of visualisation.

The five Tattvas are: *Prithivi*, a yellow square, representing the element Earth; *Apas*, a horizontal silver crescent with its tips facing upwards, representing the element Water; *Vayu*, a blue circle, representing the element Air; *Tejas*, a red triangle, representing the element Fire; and *Akasha*, a black oval, representing Spirit.

Part of the appeal of the Tattvas is that they are simple and powerful symbols for magical visualisation. According to metaphysical tradition, the Tattvas feature in the cyclic rhythm of cosmic life-energy – known as the Tattvic tide – that swirls around the planet Earth each day. *Akasha*, or Spirit, is present throughout the cycle because it encompasses all the elements, but in the flow of elemental energy *Vayu* is strongest at sunrise before merging in the middle of the day with *Tejas. Apas* then begins to come to the fore at dusk and in turn merges at midnight into *Prithivi* – and so the cycle continues.

The Tattvas are often used in magical practice as visual 'doorways' to the inner worlds of the visionary imagination, and we will explore the concept of magical 'pathworkings' later in this book. However, for the time being it will be worthwhile to concentrate on each of the Tattvas in turn, and practise holding each of these visual images in the mind's eye as meditative symbols.

It is also possible to combine each of the five elements to produce a series of sub-elements. For example, the element *Prithivi* is the densest of the five elements, and the composite form, *Prithivi of Prithivi* (Earth superimposed on Earth – a smaller yellow square superimposed over a larger yellow square), represents the densest form of all. However, if we superimpose the silver crescent of *Apas* over the yellow square of Earth we then have *Apas of Prithivi* (Water of Earth), which represents the more fluid aspect of the element Earth. If we superimpose the red triangle of Fire upon the yellow square of Earth we produce *Tejas of Prithivi* (Fire of Earth), which symbolises the molten qualities of Earth; and if we superimpose the blue circle of Air upon the yellow square of Earth we produce *Vayu of Prithivi* (Air of Earth), which diffuses or aerates the solid qualities of Earth. Finally, *Akasha of Prithivi*, a black oval superimposed over a yellow square, represents the most etheric, or spiritual, dimensions of the element Earth. As we will see later, these Tattvic combinations produce fascinating visionary results when used for magical pathworkings.[2]

But to return to the symbolic and healing qualities of colours, here are some basic colours to understand:

Red Symbolic of heat and also of the circulation of the blood, red is used by colour-healers to treat paralysis and blood ailments, and to eliminate tiredness. In the yogic Tattva system, a red triangle is the symbol for the element Fire.

Orange Symbolic of prosperity, orange is used to increase the pulse rate and to stimulate the milk-producing action of the breast after childbirth. It is also used to relieve mental fatigue and to help overcome inhibitions and shyness.

Yellow Associated with joy and happiness and also the intellect, yellow provides energy for the lymphatic system and is used to treat diabetes, indigestion, kidney and liver ailments, constipation and some throat infections. In the Tattva system, a yellow square is the symbol for the element Earth.

Green Usually applied in the emerald hue, this colour is used to treat hay fever, ulcers, influenza and colds, and also to treat nervous conditions and reduce stress. Many healers regard green as the colour of harmony because, on the rainbow spectrum, it is located midway between the warm, active colours and the cooler, passive colours.

Blue A relaxing colour, associated in some mystical systems with the throat chakra (centre of spiritual power), blue is used to alleviate pain, reduce bleeding, treat burns, dysentery, colic and respiratory problems. In the Tattva system, a blue circle is the symbol for the element Air.

Indigo This is a purifying colour, associated with the pituitary gland and the energy centre on the forehead. Therapists use this colour to treat cataracts, migraines, deafness and skin disorders. It exerts a soothing effect on the eyes, ears and nervous system.

Violet Linked to the crown chakra and the pineal gland, which is often associated with psychic and spiritual power, violet is applied in treating nervous and emotional disturbances, arthritis and sciatica. It is also used to ease childbirth.

White White light contains all the colours of the spectrum and therefore represents totality or wholeness. Luminous white light is also associated with purity, healing and spiritual transcendence. White light should be used instead of any of the individual spectral colours if you are unsure which colour to select for a particular visualisation.

There are three other colours which are not part of the rainbow spectrum but which also have profound spiritual and magical significance, and it will be worthwhile practising visualisations involving these colours as well:

Silver Silver is traditionally associated with the Moon, with reflected light and with the Universal Goddess. In the Tattva system, a horizontal silver crescent with its tips pointing upwards is the symbol for the element Water. The silver moon is also a symbol of fertility and the secret powers of Nature. Lunar goddesses in ancient religion included Isis and Hathor (Egypt), Astarte (Phoenicia), Ishtar (Babylonia), Artemis, Hecate and Selene (Greece), and Diana and Luna (Rome).

Gold Gold is traditionally associated with the Sun, with direct light and, by extension, with life itself. Gold is also a symbol of wealth and abundance. The Sun is usually personified as male, and there have been many sun-gods in ancient religion, including Ra and Osiris (Egypt); Apollo (Greece), Mithras (Persia) and Sol (Rome). In alchemy, gold is the symbol of perfection.

Black Black represents the absence of light, and because light equates with goodness, black is seen by some as representing the absence of goodness and is therefore associated with evil. However, in some spiritual traditions the colour black represents infinite, unmanifest potential – that which is yet to come forth into existence. For this reason, in the Tattva system a black oval is the symbol for the element Spirit.

HOW TO PRACTISE COLOUR BREATHING

First of all you will need to relax completely, in a way that works for you. Breathe deeply and evenly. Now select a colour and allow it to grow in your mind's eye. If the colour seems unclear or begins to blend with another colour, persist until the colour is pure and true in your inner vision. Imagine your entire body is bathed in the radiance of the colour you have chosen. Maintain a pattern of breathing deeply and rhythmically and imagine the colour being drawn into your solar plexus with each inward breath. Now visualise this specific colour spreading throughout your body, just below the skin.

A variation on this visualisation – and one which will help later on – is to practise transmitting spheres of coloured light to different parts of the body. Finally, with each outward breath, visualise any negative elements departing from your body until at last you feel cleansed and purified.

As a form of visualisation, colour breathing can help you locate different spiritual centres within your body. In Eastern meditation, these spiritual centres are best known as the chakras of Kundalini yoga. However, in the Kabbalah there are also spiritual energy centres in the body, and these are located on the so-called 'Middle Pillar' of the Tree of Life. We have already noted that the Tree of Life is a symbolic reflection of the universe as a whole and also a universal symbol of the whole human being, following the metaphysical principle 'As above, so below'. The Kabbalists believed that each of the ten spheres of consciousness could be retraced meditatively to the universal Godhead – the source of all being. They also maintained, however, that the most direct route to spiritual transcendence was to ascend via the Middle Pillar – the path of the mystic.

COLOUR VISUALISATIONS FOR THE MAGICAL ENERGY CENTRES IN THE BODY

Here are the colours associated in modern magic with the different spiritual centres located on the Middle Pillar. You might like to practise visualising these colours as spiritual energy centres in the different regions of your body:

Kabbalistic energy centre	Location	Colour
Kether	Crown of the head	Pure white
Daath*	Throat	Violet/blue
Tiphareth	Heart	Gold/yellow
Yesod	Genitals	Purple/silver
Malkuth	Feet	Russet, olive, citrine and black

* Daath – the sphere of 'Knowledge' – is sometimes referred to as the eleventh sephirah on the Tree of Life. It represents the spiritual level on the Middle Pillar which marks the crossover point between the sacred and transcendent energies of the Trinity and the energies of manifestation lower down on the Tree of Life.

Positive affirmations

It is widely recognised that affirmations assist the process of creative visualisation. So what exactly *are* affirmations, and how can we make them effective in our daily lives?

Basically, an affirmation is a confident, positive statement which you make to yourself to strengthen and reinforce your personal objectives and beliefs. Affirmations are a way of focusing your attention on specific goals and the personal attributes you would most like to acquire. They can also help to build or reinforce your self-image. In a very real way, and especially because they are essentially transformative, affirmations are a crucial component of positive everyday magic.

When you make an affirmation *you have to assume that you are already where you want to be.* Affirmations are always made in the present tense. Just as creative visualisation utilises visual imagery to evoke the here-and-now reality of an imagined situation, affirmations make use of verbal statements to overcome restrictive belief systems and to reinforce the prospect for new possibilities. As Shakti Gawain has emphasised in her work with creative visualisation, affirmations invariably have three elements: *desire* (you must truly want to change); *belief* (you must believe that change is possible); and *acceptance* (you must be willing to have the change take place). When we use affirmations in conjunction with creative visualisation we suspend disbelief by already seeing ourselves *in* the situation we are seeking, and in this way we transform the future into the present.

Here is a checklist of things to remember when making affirmations:

* Write your affirmations in the first person and in present tense so that they begin with the words 'I am' or 'I have', etc.
* Focus your affirmations on specific goals and express them in such a way that the goal is already achieved. For example: 'I am a loving person *now.*'
* Be completely positive in making your affirmation rather than including any negatives. For example, say, 'I am receiving acceptance in my life', rather than, 'I don't need this lack of acceptance in my life anymore.'
* Use words which have positive associations.
* Be specific, accurate and realistic in setting your goals.

Many people find it useful to accompany their affirmations with controlled breathing, holding the breath as the affirmation is repeated silently or aloud, and then feeling the power of the affirmation spreading through the body as the breath is released. This process should be repeated regularly to maximise the effectiveness of the affirmation.

As has been emphasised throughout this book, magic is essentially a process of visualising and attaining outcomes on different energetic levels. When we make affirmations in a magical context, we are focusing either on a physical, emotional or spiritual level in order to manifest our envisioned reality in our everyday life. Magic, then, is very much like creative visualisation except that by definition it is also able to extend beyond personal motivation into areas of profound emotional and spiritual experience.

As a means of assisting self-transformation, the most advanced form of magic, high magic, takes us into realms of consciousness which are sacred and transcendental, thereby extending our boundaries of awareness in very powerful and profound ways. But even the most basic forms of magic combine both verbal affirmations and visual imagery. The act of making affirmations in any given magical context is invariably accompanied by what I would like to refer to here as 'magical imaging'.

Magical imaging

I have chosen the term 'magical imaging' rather than 'magical imagining' for a specific reason. For many people the word 'imagining' has a suggestion of wishful thinking or fantasy about it – that is to say, a suggestion of *unreality*. And yet the true aim of all forms of magic is to envision a *different reality* and to make that reality manifest within a specific context. For this reason it seems to me more appropriate to use the word 'imaging', it having a more positive and specific thrust. Magic really is all about *imaging* because magic utilises specific images in conjunction with verbal affirmations in order to bring about a desired objective.

Earlier, when we dealt briefly with the topic of magical

aspirations, the point was made that we can make magic on any level. Magic can occur on the physical level, on an emotional level, or on a spiritual or holistic level. However, whenever and wherever magic is performed it is still operating energetically, and its effectiveness always depends on the fact that at an energetic level there are no boundaries between objects and people. If everything is interconnected at this primal level – and even quantum physics has affirmed the reality of this interconnectedness – then the magic which arises through willed intentions and envisioned outcomes is able to flow very effectively from one energy source to another. The magician's willpower and individual skill in 'imaging' simply drives the magic home to its target. It is on this level that basic spells can be surprisingly effective. Far from being simply old wives' tales or quaint folklore, spells are examples of basic magic in practice.

In his book *Spellcraft*, Robin Skelton defines a spell as 'any kind of magical act intended to have an effect upon the physical world', and I am sure most practising witches and magicians would agree with this definition. But because spells work on an energetic level they need a considerable amount of focused thought and emotion directing them.

From time to time we may become totally passionate about getting a particular job or be absolutely desperate to earn more money. If we have fallen deeply in love, or, on the downside, have become overcome by strong feelings of jealousy, competitiveness or revenge, it is likely that at certain times our emotions will know no bounds. Any spells we cast at such a time will undoubtedly have a very powerful personal energy propelling them.

If the aroused emotion is a negative one, it may be wise to pull back, if at all possible, and ask, *Do I really want to go through with this?* After all, the magic is quite likely to work! But hopefully the spell will be intended to produce a positive outcome that is beneficial to all concerned.

Here are some spells for health, love and money that you might like to try, utilising all the skills of creative visualisation, rhythmic breathing, positive affirmations and magical imaging that you have so far learned.

A SPELL FOR HEALTH

The best day to perform this spell is on a Sunday, since this day is ruled by the Sun, which brings vitality and health. Surround yourself with cheerful yellow or orange flowers, burn some marigold, ginger, rosemary or cinnamon incense, and light a golden or yellow candle. As you do this, say these words:

Sun! Sun! Shine down on me.
Pour your golden warmth over me.
Fill every cell and pore
with your life-giving radiance.
Bathe me in sunlight.
Revitalise me so your fiery essence
lifts up my spirit
and helps me shine like you do.

If the sun is shining brightly outside, bask in it for a while, or alternatively, if the day is overcast, imagine golden beams from the sun shining down and revitalising you. This spell should certainly lift your spirits and restore your sense of wellbeing. If you need to bolster the effect, repeat the spell on the following Sunday.

A SPELL FOR LOVE

Spells of love are ruled by the Goddess Venus, whose magical day is Friday.

Gather some fresh, richly scented flowers – roses, lilac, gardenias or violets are ideal – and place them in a large vase or bowl, thanking them for their gift of life as you do so. Have a small mirror handy nearby and sit or kneel in front of the bowl of flowers.

Remove one of the flowers from the bowl and stroke it lovingly over your head and across your face. At the same time, feel that you are opening yourself to the loving energy of the flower. Now close your eyes, brush the flower petals lightly across your eyelids, and say these words:

I see love.

Now, with your eyes still closed, draw the flower down a little and smell its alluring scent. Fill your spirit with its sweet aroma and say:

I breathe love.

Open your eyes, lift the flower above your head, and say:

I hold love.

Lower the flower so it is near your heart. Stroke it lovingly, feel its spiritual energies merging with yours, and say:

I feel love.

Now move the flower lower down, press it gently against

your stomach, and say:

I nourish love.

Finally, holding the flower in your hand, gaze at your reflection in the mirror, and say these words:

Love is before me,
Love is behind me,
Love is beside me,
Love is above me,
Love is below me,
Love is within me,
Love flows from me,
Love comes to me.
I am loved.

Place the bowl in a location where you can see the flowers frequently, and try to wear the particular flower you have used in your love spell. When the flower begins to discolour and wilt, bury it in the ground and thank it once again for its spiritual blessings. And now adopt a sense of emotional openness so you can truly receive love when it comes, and also be willing to give love in return.

A SPELL FOR MONEY

First ask yourself why you need the money. If the money is for a good purpose then the spell is very likely to work. In working magic, one's true motives always need to be considered.

Wait until Sunday morning, since the Sun rules material success as well as health and vitality. Light a yellow or golden candle, burn one of the money-attracting incenses like chamomile, nutmeg or myrrh, then focus your creative imagination on gold coins. Visualise this money coming into your possession for a specific purpose and also visualise as clearly as possible how it will be spent. At the same time, say these words:

> *Great Goddess of plenty,*
> *bringer of bounty,*
> *I call on you now.*
> *Listen as I ask.*
> *I need money for this purpose [focus on the purpose]*
> *Hear me,*
> *Great Goddess of plenty.*

Repeat the spell each Sunday morning until the call is answered and the money is received.

The Guardians of the Four Quarters

Already our journey along the visionary path has acquired a 'mythological' quality. Elemental spirits, for example, are found in fairy stories and legends, and personify different aspects of the universal life-force in Nature. However, as we develop our magical awareness still further we can extend upon the basic imagery of the elements and the four directions. We can finally consider the role of the Guardians of the Four Quarters, for these archetypal figures also have an important role to play in magical visualisation.[3] Although we will consider magical symbolism in more detail in the next chapter, awareness of the symbolism ascribed to the Four Quarters – the cardinal points – is a central feature in all forms of magical ritual. And because magic utilises the idea of sacred space – the space contained symbolically within a magical circle – it is hardly surprising that the magician should summon guardians to watch over this sacred space and all the ritual activities which occur within it.

Western magic provides us with four potent guardians in the form of the Archangels of the Four Elements, and it is part of effective magical practice to visualise these Archangels as protectors located at each of the cardinal points.

In the East we visualise the imposing form of Raphael, Archangel of Air. He wears a yellow cloak tinged with purple, which rustles in the wind, and we notice also that he wears winged sandals, for he is the magical counterpart of Mercury, messenger of the gods. Raphael towers high above us and holds in his hand a wand, symbol of Air.

In the South we visualise Michael, Archangel of Fire and ruler of the Sun. He wears a red cloak which flashes with sparks of green light, and his amber-coloured hair streams back from his face. In his right hand he holds aloft a flaming golden sword, symbol of Fire.

In the West we visualise Gabriel, Archangel of Water and ruler of the Moon. His cloak is silvery blue with highlights of orange, and we notice the curved crescent of the waxing moon upon his forehead. Gabriel holds aloft an overflowing silver cup, the symbol of Water.

Finally, in the North we visualise Uriel, Archangel of Earth. His robe shimmers with all the colours of Nature – traditionally represented as citrine, olive, russet and black – and he stands upon an earthen disc or pentacle, the symbol of Earth.

Soon we will learn to incorporate these four guardians into a more elaborate ritual. For the moment, though, it is important to develop the capacity to evoke the visual reality of these Archangels through magical imaging, capturing at the same time a sense of their awesome presence. This is an important step to take on the visionary path, because visualisations like this put us in touch with archetypal forces which transcend the more limited perspective of our everyday activities. Once we have begun to train ourselves in this type of visualisation we are ready to take the next step along the path. And as we will discover, this is an increasingly transformative process which will lead us steadily towards a sense of magical empowerment.

CHAPTER THREE

Sacred magic, everyday magic

All acts of magic begin with the idea of sacred space. Sacred space is where ritual is performed and spiritual events take place, where images summoned in visionary consciousness are given form and where personal transformation occurs.

The magic circle

The supreme symbol of sacred space is the magic circle, which is both a symbol of the universe as a whole and a symbol of personal spiritual endeavour. Within the sacred circle there is order, meaning, spiritual power and transformation. Beyond the sacred circle there is randomness amid the never-ending clatter and bustle of the secular world.

Magic makes use of the circle in order to define territory which is considered sacred by the practitioner. It may be a circle etched in sand, a circle drawn in the earth in a forest clearing and defined with pebbles, sticks and feathers, or a circle marked in paint or chalk on a temple floor. However, it is not the physical definition of the space itself that constitutes the power of the circle but the spiritual and emotional power that is vested in it. The circle has to be made sacred for each individual magical working. It has to have power vested in it on a continuing basis. In a spiritual sense, it has always to be made anew.

Two of the most influential approaches to magic – the ancient tradition of the Hermetic Order of the Golden Dawn and the now more dominant approach of contemporary Wicca – emphasise different symbolic aspects of the magic circle, although in essence they reflect a similar spiritual purpose.

In the Golden Dawn tradition of ceremonial magic – the tradition in which the well-known magicians Aleister Crowley and Dion Fortune were trained – the magic circle contains a *Tau* cross which, as a clearly masculine symbol, balances the feminine, womb-like symbol of the circle itself. In the Golden Dawn ceremonial circle the *Tau* cross is made up of ten squares, one for each sphere on the Kabbalistic Tree of Life, and it is vermillion in colour, as are the sacred god-names inscribed around the periphery. The circle area itself is green. Nine equidistantly placed pentagrams, each containing a small glowing lamp, surround the circle, and a tenth – the most important – hangs above the centre as a symbol of mystical aspiration. The circle must be large enough for the ritual magician to move around in, and the magician must always remain within the circle during a magical invocation, for to leave it mid-ceremony would destroy its power as a focus for the magical will and as a circle of 'psychic' protection.

In terms of construction, where the circle is not a perma-nent fixture of the temple floor it can be chalked in colour or, alternatively, sewn or printed on cloth. As we noted ear-lier, whenever the circle is already in existence its sacred nature must always be reaffirmed in the consciousness of the magician at the beginning of each ritual, for the circle would otherwise remain a secular symbol. To reaffirm the spiritual significance of the magic circle the magician therefore traces over its inscribed form with a ceremonial sword or out-stretched hand, at the same time carefully reflecting on the meaning of this symbolic action.

In the Wiccan tradition, which of course focuses primari-ly on the Universal Goddess, the magic circle has heightened significance. In Wicca it is regarded as a symbol of the womb of the Goddess herself, representing containment, totality and a sense of transcendent wholeness. The well-known neo-pagan writer Margot Adler calls the sacred circle a 'micro-cosm of the universe', and Wiccan devotee Starhawk says that the magic circle 'exists on the boundaries of ordinary space and time [for] it is "between the worlds" of the seen and unseen ... a space in which alternate realities meet, in which the past and future are open to us.'[1]

In Wicca the magic circle is usually marked by the four cardinal points, and these in turn are linked to the four ele-ments. As with the Guardians of the Four Quarters referred to in the previous chapter, in Wicca the direction north is associated with Earth (symbolising the physical body), east with Air (associated with thoughts and communication), south with Fire (energy and will), and west with Water (emo-tions and feelings). The centre of the circle represents Spirit, for in Spirit (the fifth essence, or quintessence) we find a resolution of the four elements and a true sense of unity.

Wiccan ceremony is more spontaneous and less complex than the magic of the Golden Dawn, and many Wiccan rituals begin by simply drawing the magic circle with a stick or with chalk. Alternatively, one may stand within an existing circle, if a special space has already been prepared. However, as in the Golden Dawn, the circle has to be marked off ritually, distinguishing the sacred space that will be the focus of the ritual. The four elements are then invoked at the cardinal points, followed by invocations to the Goddess.

Wiccans working in groups also focus on the image of the magic circle to build what they call 'the cone of power' – a vortex of collective magical energy which can be directed towards the specific ritual at hand. In building the cone of power, members of the group run clockwise around the circle holding hands, at the same time focusing their attention on the central altar candle. Often this is accompanied by 'the Witches' Rune', a colourful chant written by Gerald Gardner and Doreen Valiente, which has since become part of international Wiccan folklore:

Eko, Eko Azarak
Eko, Eko Zamilak
Eko, Eko, Cernunnos
Eko, Eko, Aradia
Darkesome night and shining moon
East, then South, then West, then North;
Hearken to the Witches' Rune –
Here we come to call ye forth!
Earth and water, air and fire,
Wand and pentacle and sword,
Work ye unto our desire,

Hearken ye unto our word!
Cords and censer, scourge and knife,
Powers of the witch's blade –
Waken all ye into life,
Come ye as the charm is made!
Queen of heaven, Queen of hell,
Horned hunter of the night –
Lend your power unto the spell,
And work our will by magic rite!
By all the power of land and sea,
By all the might of moon and sun –
As we do will, so mote it be;
Chant the spell, and be it done!
Eko, Eko Azarak
Eko, Eko Zamilak
Eko, Eko, Cernunnos
Eko, Eko, Aradia.

We can now consider some of the other magical symbols from the Golden Dawn and Wiccan traditions.

The Golden Dawn tradition

In the Golden Dawn tradition, the magic temple represents the entire universe. By extension it also represents the individual figure of the magician (because of the relationship between the macrocosm and the microcosm as expressed in the Hermetic concept 'As above, so below'). Mounted on the walls of the temple are banners emblazoned with sacred symbols and colours appropriate to the magical imagery of the ritual[2], and on the floor of the temple are certain inscriptions, the most important of which relate to the magic circle. In the Golden Dawn tradition the circle represents the Infinite Godhead – the Alpha and Omega, the state of spiritual awareness and transcendence to which the magician aspires. By standing in the centre of the circle, the magician is able to identify with the sacred source of Creation and his magical will is oriented totally towards the spheres of higher spiritual aspiration. As a symbol of what the magician may become, the circle also symbolises the process of magical invocation itself – the act of reaching towards a higher spiritual reality by identifying with a goddess or a god.[3]

Several magical implements are also employed by the magician within the circle. Most of these objects are placed upon the central altar, which symbolises the foundation of the ritual itself. Consisting of a double cube of wood – traditionally made of acacia or oak – the altar has ten exposed faces, corresponding with the ten sephiroth on the Tree of Life. The lowest face is Malkuth (the Kingdom, or the World), which represents things as they are in the manifested universe. The upper face represents Kether (the Crown), the highest sphere upon the Tree of Life.

Placed upon the magical altar are certain symbolic implements designed to channel the imagination of the magician towards transcendence. These are:

The holy oil This golden fluid is ideally contained in a vessel of rock-crystal. In using it, the magician anoints the Four Points of the Microcosm (Kether, Chesed, Geburah and Malkuth) on his forehead, left and right shoulders and solar plexus respectively, at the same time reflecting on the sacred task ahead. The holy ointment traditionally consists of the oils of olive, myrrh, cinnamon and galangual, these corresponding in turn to Chokmah (Wisdom), Binah (Understanding), Tiphareth (Harmony/ Spiritual Awakening) and Kether-Malkuth (the Union of Being and Creation on the Tree of Life).

The wand This implement symbolises the pursuit of Higher Wisdom (Chokmah), achieved through the Will. Symbolically, the tip of the wand is said to rest in Kether, the first sephirah of the Tree of Life, which contains the Union of Opposites and represents the transcendence of duality in all its forms. A multicoloured lotus wand is used, its upper end white and its lower end black. The white end is used for magical invocation, the black end for 'banishing' or removing malevolent forces. In between the white and black ends of the wand are twelve bands of colour corresponding to the different signs of the zodiac:

Red	Aries
Red-orange	Taurus
Orange	Gemini
Amber	Cancer
Lemon-yellow	Leo
Yellow-green	Virgo
Emerald	Libra
Green-blue	Scorpio
Blue	Sagittarius
Indigo	Capricorn
Violet	Aquarius
Purple	Pisces

The wand represents the first letter, Yod, of the Tetragrammaton JHVH (Jehovah – the sacred name of God), and also the element Air.[4] The other ritual magical implements described here – the cup, sword and disc (also known as the pentacle) complete the sacred name of God and represent the elements Water, Fire and Earth respectively.

The cup As a feminine, receptive symbol, the cup is associated with Binah, the Mother of Understanding. The magician believes he must fill his cup of consciousness with an understanding and knowledge of his Higher Self. As a symbol of *containment* rather than of *becoming*, the cup is not used in rituals of invocation but in ceremonies related to acts of manifestation.

The sword Indicative of the magician's mastery over evoked and invoked powers, the sword, which symbolises human force, parallels the wand, which represents divine power. Suggestive of control and order, the sword is the 'offspring' of Wisdom and Understanding (Chokmah and Binah) and is therefore attributed to Tiphareth, the sphere of harmony. The symmetry of the sword is correspondingly appropriate. According to Aleister Crowley, the guard should consist of two moons waxing and waning, affixed to the back (Yesod), and the blade should be made of steel (corresponding to Mars). The hilt should be constructed of copper (the metal symbolically associated with Venus), indicating that ultimately the sword is subject to the rule of love. When the sword is placed symbolically on the Tree of Life, the pommel rests in Daath – the 'sphere' associated with the Abyss beneath the Trinity – and the points of the guard lie in Chesed and Geburah. The tip rests in Malkuth. Crowley makes the observation that 'the Magician cannot wield the Sword unless the Crown is on his head.' That is to say, force and aspiration without spiritual inspiration are finally of no avail.

The disc (pentacle) In the same way that the sword is paired with the wand, both being symbolically masculine, the disc is paired with the cup as a feminine symbol. Symbolic of Malkuth, the Heavenly Daughter and goddess of the manifest universe, the disc is said traditionally to 'induce awe' in the consciousness of the magician. Malkuth represents the first step on the mystical journey back to the Source of All Being. It also represents the consciousness of the magician *prior* to spiritual illumination.

The ceremonial magician wears on his head the **crown**, or headband, representative of Kether. Golden in colour, it is a symbol of aspiration towards the Divine. Over the magician's body falls the **robe**, which serves as a protection against adverse 'astral' influences. Hooded, and normally black in colour, the robe symbolises anonymity and silence and is the dark vessel into which the light of the spirit will be poured. Attached to it, or sewn across the chest, is the lamen or breastplate, which protects the heart (Tiphareth). And in the same way that Tiphareth is the focal point of all the sephiroth because of its central position upon the Tree of Life, the Lamen has inscribed upon it symbols which relate to all aspects of the magical purpose. Considered an 'active' form of the passive disc, the lamen indicates strength. So too does the magical book, which the magician holds in his hands. This book contains all the details of one's ritual aims and practice, and in a sense represents the unfolding 'history' of the magical will. As such, the magical book is a symbol of personal power and resolve.

In addition, the ceremonial magician sometimes employs the use of a **bell**, worn on a chain around the neck. Representative of a state of alertness, it is said to be the bell which sounds 'at the elevation of the Host', a reference to the sublime music of the higher spheres. In this respect the symbolism of the bell parallels that of the **sacred lamp**, which as 'the light of the pure soul' is positioned above the ritual implements on the altar and represents the descent of spirit into form, and light into darkness. It stands for all that is eternal and unchanging and also represents the first swirlings of the primal energy which gave rise to the Universe ('Let there be Light ...').

The magical tools of Wiccan ritual

In Wiccan ceremonies, most witches work 'sky-clad', or naked. However, robes are often worn by the High Priest and High Priestess as a sign of symbolic rank during major initiations, and there are some neopagan groups whose members prefer to work fully robed at all times.

As with the magic of the Golden Dawn, certain magical implements define the very nature of Wiccan ritual practice. On the witch's altar, the chalice represents the element Water, salt represents Earth and the censer both Air and Fire. The pentacle represents Earth and is also used as a receptacle for the 'mooncakes' which are eaten in communion at the close of the ritual. Also on the altar are the communion wine, an altar candle and the witch's personal tools and 'weapons'. The basic implements of witchcraft are as follows:

The sword This is a symbol of power and authority and is used to cast the circle. It is also a potent symbol of protection.

The athame This double-edge black-handled knife – sometimes with symbols on its hilt – is used to direct magical power. It can also be used to cast the magic circle. The athame should ideally have an iron blade representing the will and an ebony handle representing steadfastness. A white-handled knife called a **boline** may also be located on the altar, but its use is purely utilitarian. The **dagger** is employed in ceremonial rites for invoking and banishing spirits.

The cup or chalice This is a ritual object associated with the element Water and is also a symbol of the womb of the Goddess. When the athame is inserted into a chalice filled with liquid it represents the sacred marriage of the God and Goddess: 'As the athame is to the male, so the chalice is to the female, and when conjoined become one.' The cup is also used as a receptacle for the ritual wine.

The wand Used to direct the will and to summon and control spirits the wand must be held with both hands with its point well away from the body. It is usually made from willow, birch, hazel, oak or elder. Wiccans go into the woods to find an appropriate piece of wood which can then be fashioned into a wand.

The brass thurible Standing on three legs or hanging from three chains, this is the container for the incense. In Wiccan ceremonies it is taken around the edge of the circle to purify the sacred space with the elements of Fire and Air.

The disc or pentacle This is a symbol of the element Earth. It is used to call earth spirits and may also be used to cast the magic circle by rolling the disc around the circumference.

The three-pronged candelabra Depending on the nature of the lunar cycle or the nature of the ritual itself, the candelabra will contain a white candle (the Goddess as maiden), a red candle (the Goddess as mother) or a black candle (the Goddess as crone). The black candle represents age and wisdom and is not a symbol of the 'black arts'.

The altar cloth Usually black or white the altar cloth has resting upon it containers for both the salt and water which are used to purify the circle with the elements Earth and Water. Some altars also display small figurines of specific goddesses and gods considered appropriate to the specific ritual in question.

Other items employed in Wiccan rites include the **besom**, a broom fashioned from six different woods (birch, broom, hawthorn, hazel, rowan and willow) which is used to clean the ritual area, and the **cauldron**, a female symbol made of cast iron. It has three legs, representing the three faces of the Goddess (maiden, mother and crone), and is used to generate a safe ceremonial fire during indoor rituals. Every witch also needs a **book of shadows**. This is the witch's personal collection of rituals, spells, herbal remedies and other details of occult lore. Sometimes a **scourge** is also used in Wiccan rituals. Intended primarily as an aid to spiritual purification in initiation ceremonies, it is generally used for mild forms of self-flagellation and is only rarely used for punishing offenders within the coven.

As we have said, most Wiccans like to work sky-clad in their magical ceremonies. However, in groups where robes are worn, the specific colours and symbolic embellishments are likely to vary considerably. The most common ritual attire is a black hooded robe, large enough to allow ample room for movement and dancing. High Priests and High

Priestesses are often robed during major initiations and may choose to wear symbolically coloured cords around their waists. This cord is called the **cingulum** and is traditionally 3 feet 6 inches (125 cm) long, to ensure that a traditional witches' circle of at least 9 feet (275 cm) diameter can be easily measured. The cingulum may also be used when candidates are ritually bound during initiation ceremonies.

A final point should be made about Wiccan ritual, and that is that the four basic elements are celebrated in distinct but complementary ways. The element Earth is honoured through the ritual use of salt, Water through the use of essential oils, Fire by lighting candles of different symbolic colours, and Air through the use of different types of incense. On the next page is a table which refers to the magical applications of the principal magical oils and incenses, as well as to the symbolic qualities of different coloured candles.

The nature of ritual

On one level, all forms of ceremonial ritual are a type of theatrical performance, but they always relate to an inner process as well. In all forms of magical expression – from ancient shamanism to contemporary Wicca – anyone performing a ritual believes that what they are doing relates to some sort of sacred, inner reality. For a time, the participant in the ritual will feel caught up in a mystical drama, perhaps involving union with a goddess or a god, identification with a source of spiritual healing or the act of embodying some sort of transcendent power. In this way the person engaging in the ritual is tappng into a dimension which is much larger and more awesome than the world of familiar everyday reality.

Some rituals lead us towards a sense of transcendence

ESSENTIAL OILS	MAGICAL APPLICATION (WATER ELEMENT)
Bergamot	For protection and attracting money
Cedarwood	For restoring health
Chamomile	For harmony, relaxation and healing
Cinnamon	For attracting lovers and good luck
Frankincense	For spiritual power and clairvoyance
Geranium	For restoring health and increasing one's ability to take risks
Jasmine	For luck, success and romantic love
Lavender	To soothe and bring peace
Lemon	To banish negative energies
Musk	To arouse erotic desire
Myrrh	For inspiration and spiritual awareness
Orange	To heighten intuitive and psychic powers
Patchouli	For financial gain and to arouse passion
Peppermint	For personal protection
Pine	To purify and banish negativity
Rose	For luck and love
Rosemary	For protection and to enhance learning and memory
Sandalwood	To heighten intuition and clairvoyance
Verbena	For strength and resilience

* * * * * *

PLANETARY RULERS	MAGICAL INCENSES (AIR ELEMENT)
The Sun	Frankincense, olibanum, wood-aloes
The Moon	Jasmine, camphor
Mercury	Sandalwood
Venus	Rosewood, benzoin
Mars	Pine flowers, thistles, nettles, tobacco
Jupiter	Cedar, oakmoss, balm
Saturn	Myrrh, alum

MAGIC CANDLES	SYMBOLIC QUALITIES (FIRE ELEMENT)
White	For spirituality, peace and purification
Red	For strength, energy, courage and sexual passion
Pink	For love, tenderness and romantic affection
Orange	For health, ambition and matters pertaining to the law
Yellow	For intellect, memory and mental abilities
Green	For harmony, abundance, good fortune and fertility
Blue	For inspiration, wisdom and devotion
Purple	To heighten spiritual and psychic awareness
Silver	For intuition and psychic inspiration
Gold	To attract wealth, abundance and prosperity
Brown	For special favours and to dispel sorrow
Black	Symbolic of old age and wisdom

while others involve major rites of passage. Whatever the circumstance, we can recognise that any particular magical ritual should be a *transformative* experience. As one American neopagan practitioner has expressed it: 'I want to learn something, I want to be moved, I want to feel renewed, I want to feel like I've had some sort of participation in something bigger than myself.'[5]

It is also widely acknowledged in Wiccan circles that 'good ritual' doesn't just happen by itself. It involves a blend of effective planning and spontaneity, a mix of balanced intent and inspiration. Like a good story, a ritual should also have a beginning, a middle and an end. Wisconsin-based witch Selena Fox similarly divides rituals into three parts: preparation and orientation; the work or focus of the ritual itself; and the closure and assimilation.[6] Wiccans recognise that sacred energy must be 'grounded' at the close of a ritual, thereby enabling participants to return to the 'real' world of everyday activities. Sometimes a group will share cakes and wine as part of the closure, and there will also be a parting blessing: 'The circle is open but never broken. Merry meet, merry part, and merry meet again ...'

Creating a sacred space

Our first practical step now is to create a sacred space. This involves defining the magic circle itself, 'banishing' the impure elements within it, then reinforcing the sense of magical protection at the cardinal points. The best ritual I know for doing this is the Banishing Ritual of the Pentagram, and it includes references to the Guardians of the Four Directions referred to in the last chapter.

I should mention here that the magical symbol of the pentagram – a five-pointed star – represents the five elements, Earth, Fire, Water, Air and Spirit. The pentagram itself is also a symbol of a human being standing with arms outstretched. When the apex of the triangle reaches upwards the pentagram is indicating that our magical aspirations are directed towards the element Spirit, and the pentagram then becomes a symbol of white magic – the magic of spiritual intent. When the apex of the triangle faces downwards, the pentagram is pointing away from the element Spirit and the pentagram then becomes a symbol of black magic.[7]

We begin by standing in silence in the chosen location. Our first action is to perform the exercise known as the

Kabbalistic Cross. The Kabbalistic Cross exercise is designed to strengthen our magical sense of self and can be used to commence any magical ritual.

Imagine that pure white light is descending from above and entering your forehead. Hold the vibrancy of this white light in your conscious awareness; touch your forehead with the pointed fingers of your right hand, and then intone the word *Ateh* (pronounced 'Ah-teh'), which means 'Thou art'. Now visualise that you are drawing the white light down with your fingers into your breast and intone the word *Malkuth* (pronounced ' Mal-kooth'). *Malkuth* means 'the Kingdom' and represents the lowest sphere on the Tree of Life. Now use your pointed fingers and your powers of visualisation to draw the white light across to your right shoulder and intone *Ve Geburah* ('Vay-geb-or-ah'), which means 'and the Power'. Then draw the light across to your left shoulder and intone *Ve Gedulah* ('Vay-ged-yu-lah'), which means 'and the Glory'. Close by drawing your hands over your chest and intone *Le Olahm* ('Lay-oh-lahm'), Amen. 'Le Olahm' means 'to the ages'. This concludes the first stage of the procedure.

The next step in creating a sacred magic circle will involve using your powers of magical imaging to create a ring of luminous astral fire around the chosen space, demarcating this space at the four cardinal points with flaming white-light pentagrams.

Because you are clearing a sacred space on the earth or floor of a temple, you commence with the Earthen tip of the pentagram (that is, the lower left tip). At each of the four chief points of the compass, create the magical image of the pentagram directly in front of you, at shoulder height.

Begin by facing east and using your outstretched arm to

delineate a large pentagram immediately in front of you, commencing at the lower left-hand corner and then proceeding clockwise to complete the shape of the five-pointed star. Visualise that you are creating a pentagram of luminous fire. Draw your hand back after you have completed it, take an in-breath, and now with a piercing gesture thrust your pointed hand forward into the centre of the pentagram. Now, with an extended out-breath, vibrate 'JHVH' (pronounced 'Ye-ho-waaa'), the sacred god-name for the element Air.

Now turn towards the south and visualise as you turn that a potent arc of flame is now extending from the pentagram in the east around to this new position in the south. Once again, create the pentagram of luminous fire in front of you, but this time as you make the thrusting gesture towards the centre of the pentagram vibrate 'ADNI' (pronounced 'Aaa-Doh-naiii'), the sacred god-name for the element Fire.

Face west and continue creating the circle of light as before. This time you should vibrate 'EHIEH' (pronounced 'Eee-Hee-Yeh') through the pentagram thus speaking the sacred god-name for the element Water.

Now as you face north you will complete the final pentagram. This time vibrate 'AGLA' (pronounced 'Aaa-glaaa'), the sacred God name for the element Earth. Then complete the circle of fire by extending it around to the east, closing the circle at the point where you commenced.

You have now succeeded in placing four protective pentagrams of fire at each of the four cardinal points and you have created a circle of luminous white light. Now you are in a position to summon each of the four guardian Archangels in turn.

Facing first towards the east, hold your arms outstretched

like the arms of a cross. Visualise each of these guardians surrounding you (the visualisations for Raphael, Gabriel, Michael and Uriel were provided at the end of the previous chapter) and invoke each of the Archangels in turn:

Before me Raphael ('Raa-fay-el')
Behind me Gabriel ('Gab-ray-el')
On my right hand Michael ('Mee-kay-el')
On my left hand Uriel ('Or-ray-el')
For about me flames the Pentagram
And above me shines the six-rayed star [8]

Having created the sacred space and reinforced it psychically with protective pentagrams and a circle of fire, you are now in a position to conduct the specific ritual you have in mind, which may be an invocation to a specific god or goddess, or a magical visualisation directed towards the astral planes of visionary consciousness. Sybil Leek's invocation to the Lunar Goddess to celebrate the rebirth of the Sun from the depths of winter provides us with an excellent example of how to call upon the higher spiritual powers who rule Heaven and Earth:

Queen of the Moon,
Queen of the Stars,
Queen of the Horns,
Queen of the Fires,
Queen of the Earth,
Bring to us the Child of Promise!
For it is the Great Mother
Who gives birth to the new year,
Darkness and tears are set aside,

When the Sun comes up again,
Golden Sun of hill and mountain,
Illumine the world,
Illumine the seas,
Illumine the rivers,
Illumine us all.
Grief be laid and joy be raised,
Blessed by the Great Mother!
Without beginning, without end,
Everlasting to Eternity.
Evoe! Evoe! Io! [9]

Becoming the goddess or the god

Ultimately, most forms of magic involve identifying closely with a goddess or a god – or even *becoming* a goddess or god. This may seem like an arrogant or pretentious idea, but the basic principle is to seek to embody the spiritual qualities which the goddess or god represents. The idea is then to bring these sacred qualities through into one's daily life so that even common, everyday events are in some degree enriched or transformed.

Considered in this light, gods and goddesses personify particular idealised attributes – qualities which we would like to acquire. To this extent, gods and goddesses are archetypes of what we ourselves would like to become.

The act of identifying magically with a goddess or a god is known in the Golden Dawn tradition as 'assuming the god-form'. This means that within the sacred context of a magical ritual the individual invokes and seeks to absorb the attributes and qualities of that particular deity into his or her own being. He or she does so with such a degree of intensity that a type of miraculous fusion of identities takes place. This, of course, requires a considerable amount of mental and emotional effort, and also an extensive amount of prior study of the gods and goddesses of ancient religious and mythological pantheons. However, simply researching the details of a particular god or goddess in world mythology will not necessarily summon the *essence* of that deity, since invoking an archetypal being within the context of a magical ritual takes place on an energetic level and is not just an intellectual endeavour. Neither can we regard the act of 'assuming the god-form' simply as an exercise in creative visualisation, for it becomes much more than that. This particular type of magic involves a fusion of human and sacred consciousness.

High magic provides us with the keys for this type of spiritual fusion, with some branches of the magical tradition proving more appropriate than others in this regard. The Kabbalistic Tree of Life is of little relevance here, the Tree of Life belonging to the Jewish spiritual tradition which is monotheistic. From a monotheistic perspective, the different archetypal spheres upon the Tree of Life and their associated sacred god-names are all considered as aspects of the One God rather than as a group of individual deities. However, other mythic traditions – for example, the pantheons of ancient Egypt, Greece, Rome and Celtic Europe – provide us with groupings of specific gods and goddesses, each of whom were believed to embody individual qualities. The best known of these in the West are probably the Greco-Roman gods and goddesses, because they have become accessible to us through their association with the planets and popular astrology. Here are some of the more familiar deities from ancient Greece and Rome, together with their symbolic attributes:

* Apollo, god of the Sun, associated with healing, music and poetry as well as ambition and success.
* Diana/Artemis/Selene/Hecate, goddess of the Moon, protector of girls and young women, and also associated with hunting and all animal species. As the lunar goddess, she is also closely associated with the night-time, with dreams, and with the powers of the imagination.
* Mercury/Hermes, the messenger of the gods, associated with oratory, athletics and affairs of trade. As god of the wind, he also conducts the souls of the dead to the Underworld. Mercury is associated with memory, intelligence, education and communication.
* Venus/Aphrodite, goddess of love and beauty, sexual love and desire, and relationships in general. She also represents prosperity and good luck. Astrologers associate Venus with harmony and affection, as well as with music and the arts.
* Mars/Aries, god of war, associated with strong personal willpower and courage as well as with all forms of violence, hostility and aggression.
* Jupiter/Zeus, father of the gods and ruler of Heaven and Earth, regarded as wise, all-knowing and merciful. He is also revered as the god of thunder and lightning and is associated with optimism, happiness and abundance, as well as with material wealth and political power.
* Saturn/Kronos, god of time, agriculture and the harvest but also associated with solitude, the elderly, ill health and death.

You may wish to create your own personal rituals to honour a specific goddess or a god (for details of the symbolic attributes of particular deities please refer to the Table of Magical

Correspondences at the back of this book). Meanwhile, an excellent example of magical invocation and 'assuming the god-form' is found in contemporary Wicca, where the High Priestess of the coven seeks to embody the sacred qualities of the Universal Goddess. This takes place during the ritual invocation of 'Drawing Down the Moon'.

Drawing Down the Moon

The invocation of Drawing Down the Moon plays a very important role in contemporary Wiccan ritual. Here the High Priest calls the Goddess into the High Priestess as part of the opening ceremony:

> *I invoke Thee and beseech Thee, O Mighty Mother of all life and fertility. By seed and root, by stem and bud, by leaf and flower and fruit, by life and Love do I invoke Thee to descend into the body of this thy servant and High Priestess.*[10]

Once the High Priestess has incarnated the Goddess, she then utters what is known in Wicca as the Charge. Here, in effect, the Goddess herself is speaking directly to her followers. But first the High Priest addresses the coven:

> *Listen to the words of the Great Mother; she who of old was called among men Artemis, Astarte, Athene, Dione, Melusine, Aphrodite, Cerridwen, Dana, Arianrhod, Isis, Bride, and by many other names.*

The High Priestess now speaks to the group as the Goddess incarnate:

> *Whenever ye have need of anything, once in the month, and*

better it be when the moon is full, then shall ye assemble in some secret place and adore the spirit of me, who am Queen of all witches. There shall ye assemble, ye who are fain to learn all sorcery, yet who have not won its deepest secrets; to these will I teach things that are yet unknown. And ye shall be free from slavery; and as a sign that ye be really free, ye shall be naked in your rites; and ye shall dance, sing, feast, make music and love, all in my praise. For mine is the ecstasy of the spirit, and mine is also joy on earth; for my law is love unto all beings. Keep pure your highest ideal; strive ever towards it; let naught stop you or turn you aside. For mine is the secret door which opens up the Land of Youth, and mine is the cup of the wine of life, and the Cauldron of Cerridwen, which is the Holy Grail of immortality. I am the gracious Goddess, who gives the gift of joy unto the heart of man. Upon earth, I give the knowledge of the spirit eternal; and beyond death, I give peace, and freedom, and reunion with those who have gone before. Nor do I demand sacrifice; for behold, I am the mother of all living, and my love is poured out upon the earth.

The High Priest now briefly intercedes:

Hear ye the words of the Star Goddess; she in the dust of whose feet are the hosts of heaven, and whose body encircles the universe.

And then, once again, the Goddess addresses the coven through the High Priestess:

I who am the beauty of the green earth, and the white Moon among the stars, and the mystery of the waters, and the desire of the heart of man, call unto thy soul. Arise and come unto me. For I am the soul of Nature, who gives life to the universe. From me all things proceed, and unto me all things must return; and before my face, beloved of Gods and men, let thine innermost divine self be enfolded in the rapture of the infinite. Let my worship be within the heart that rejoiceth; for behold all acts of love and pleasure are my rituals. And therefore let there be beauty and strength, power and compassion, honour and humility, mirth and reverence within you. And thou who thinkest to seek for me, know that seeking and yearning shall avail thee not unless thou knowest the mystery; that if that which thou seekest thou findest not within thee, thou wilt never find it without thee. For behold, I have been with thee from the beginning; and I am that which is attained at the end of desire.[11]

The power of the sacred word

Both in the Golden Dawn and Wiccan traditions, magical ritual invariably involves the invocation of spiritual beings or archetypal forces through the potency of the spoken word, and this also relates strongly to the idea of *will*, which distinguishes magic from the more passive forms of conventional religion.

In most magical groups, members are given special new names – names which remain secret, except to their magical colleagues – to mark the different stages of magical initiation. This is based on the idea that magical names do not just consist of ordinary words but identify *who we really are*. They are really part of our essence and identify us on an energetic level. A magical name is often a statement of magical purpose as well. In the Golden Dawn,

EVERYDAY MAGIC

Aleister Crowley took the magical name *Perdurabo*, meaning 'I will endure to the end'. For him, this was quite intentional: 'Words should express will,' he said, 'hence the Mystic Name of the Probationer is the expression of his highest Will.'[12]

What emerges from this is that, in magic, sound – and also magical names – are often regarded as a source of sacred power, and our magical name then becomes a reflection of our personal identity and our true purpose upon the visionary path. Magicians keep their magical names secret in order to protect their sacred source of inner strength.

Personal power

Whatever sense of personal power we hold as a reflection of our self-esteem, our individual sense of worth and our personal effectiveness, there is always room to develop our potential still further. Our personal power can be measured not only through the way we relate to others but also by how we regard ourselves, and how strong we feel in a holistic sense – not only physically, but also emotionally and spiritually. From a magical perspective, personal power encompasses all levels of our being and places greater emphasis on power aligned with the spiritual will; power which accords with a sense of greater purpose.

It is up to each of us as individual human beings to determine what our 'greater purpose' actually is, and this idea is reflected in the concept of the magical will. On a practical level, what we are calling 'will' is all about personal intent – about what we do in any given situation. However, on a metaphysical level it has to do with following a purpose which is aligned not only with our physical activities but also

104

with our mental, emotional and spiritual potential. Aligning ourselves with our true sense of spiritual purpose used to be called 'communing with our Holy Guardian Angel', but this suggests a spiritual or transcendental entity outside of ourselves. Nowadays we can think of it more in terms of tapping our sacred inner potential. This means literally getting in touch with the highest and most sacred dimensions of our being, for it is at this spiritual level that we are directly connected with the Universe as a whole.

From a magical point of view, this is the most profound meaning of 'personal power'. This is not a concept of ego-based power – the sort of power one can use to dominate or manipulate other people in our daily lives. It is more the sort of power which recognises a shared unity of purpose. This sense of purpose only comes about when we are able to sense the bigger picture and regard ourselves in an expanded, and yet more inclusive, human and spiritual context.

Magic has a lot to offer in this regard because it is essentially teaching us an archetypal way of living our lives. The various classical pantheons of ancient religion – the gods and goddesses of the Greco-Roman, Egyptian and Celtic cultures, and so on – provide us with structures for personal spiritual growth. By performing our magical rituals and by developing our capacity for new visionary perspectives we begin to reformulate our individual lives on a mythic or magical level, and we come to see the world in a new way. Some have called this 're-sacralising the world', which means bringing a sacred quality to our everday lives. This is a concept of personal power and spiritual alignment which reaches down into our day-to-day lives; an approach which allows everyday magic to come alive for us, both at home and in our work.

Magic at home

Our home is very much an extension of ourselves. It is usually the place where we live with the people we love most, where we feel safe and protected from the outside world, and where we have our focus in everyday life. Our home is also our own personal universe: an expression of our creativity, our sensitivity to colour and decoration, and the place where we keep many of our most prized possessions. Across a broad spectrum of styles and personal tastes, our home sends a message about our personal identity. So if we are following a magical path, it won't be at all surprising if our home reflects this as well, for in this realm, as in so many others, the microcosm is a mirror of the macrocosm.

Traditionally, the home is said to be ruled by the Moon. Just like the magical circle in Wicca, the home is a miniature version of the womb of the Universal Goddess. It is our own personal universe and our own personal creation. While in most cases it is unrealistic to expect that our entire house can become a temple, especially if we are sharing it with others who may have different spiritual beliefs from those we hold ourselves, we should nevertheless find a place within our home which can become our own sacred space. This then becomes a space dedicated to spiritual practice, meditation, visualisation or 'quiet time' generally.

This special space should be ritually cleansed on a regular basis, for it will be a place where we may choose to erect our own personal altar, with all the associated magical implements and symbolic images that accompany our spiritual practice. Indeed, many Wiccans I know cleanse their entire houses ritually on a regular basis – and by this I mean psychically as well as physically. The idea is to eliminate any negative energetic vibrations from one's own sacred space.

When we are living in the city, as most of us are, the collective thought-forms of the urban population are definitely a force to contend with!

So in establishing a magical space at home, or if you are moving into a new house, it is always a good idea to conduct a ritual cleansing. This is best done at the time of new moon or full moon, when the energies of the Goddess are at their peak. Some people like to sprinkle a few crystals of sea salt or drops of salted water around the periphery of each room, since salt, as the element for Earth, provides symbolic protection. It is also a good idea to burn incense in each room as a symbolic purification through the element Fire. And in the room you have selected for your own spiritual practice it will be vital to perform your own cleansing or 'psychic banishing' ritual. The Banishing Ritual of the Pentagram described earlier (see pages 94–97) will certainly be effective in this regard, but if you incline more towards the Wiccan path there are also very effective Wiccan rituals for banishing and purification.[13] Many Wiccans like to keep small clusters of sacred herbs in different corners of the home. Angelica is a good choice because it represents peace and harmony. Visualising a circle of invisibility around your home and pronouncing it invisible to all forms of evil is also to be recommended.[14]

Once you have established a sacred space it is appropriate to have your own personal blessing ceremony in order to give thanks to the Goddess or any other protective deity for what you have received. At this time you may also like to install a symbolic 'household guardian' in your home. We have a beautifully crafted wooden Thunderbird in our home – acquired during a trip to the Canadian north-west – and he guards the entrance to our living area very effectively!

As well as lighting candles, burning incense or heating essential oils in a diffuser on a regular basis, it is a good idea to surround yourself with plants and flowers from your garden. This brings the healing fragrance of flowers and herbs into the home. Meanwhile, you can hang wind chimes outside where the breeze will catch them. This honours the element Air and also provides wonderful spontaneous melodies from Nature herself.

Some people also feel it is a good idea to paint the front door of one's home in an appropriate symbolic colour, especially since the front door represents the portal between your inner, personal world and the world outside. Extrovert personalities often incline towards the brighter, more vibrant colours, while introverts may prefer cooler, more soothing tones. This is obviously very much a matter of individual choice, and you may like to refer back to the section on the symbolism of different colours described in the previous chapter.

Magic in the workplace

Where you work is very different from where you live. Obviously it is a secular environment, not a sacred space, and the people you are working with may have very different career aspirations, personal beliefs and ideas of personal power from yours. It is quite likely that their personal agendas will be different as well. If you work in an office with a hierarchical power structure, it is very common to encounter highly ambitious, sometimes ruthless individuals who are desperate to ascend the corporate ladder. Having worked in private enterprise myself for nearly 25 years, I have seen this all too clearly. The global marketplace is becoming ever more competitive and aggressive, and one has to have a securely defined sense of self-worth to survive, let alone to get ahead, in a corporate sense. Unfortunately, our society tends to reward those who most strongly project their egoic personas within the office or workplace environment, and as we mentioned earlier this may have little or nothing to do with one's spiritual purpose in life. Indeed, it is common to find that spiritually inclined people often try to keep their workplace environment and their inner spiritual life completely separate. One's regular work is then regarded as something which takes place well and truly outside the magic circle and does not belong within the sacred inner sanctum.

Obviously you cannot make your office into a temple or 'sacred space'. However, I think it is possible to decorate your office with motifs, colours and symbols which reflect your personality and individuality and which send a message to your work colleagues that says you are a person with flair and imagination and that you have a positive contribution to make. This also shows in the clothes or jewellery you choose to wear. While the colour black continues to dominate fashions in the workplace, try introducing a few magical 'power colours' into your wardrobe as well: bold reds, oranges and yellows, or metaphysical indigos and purples. Every now and then, select unconventional colour combinations to demonstrate your capacity for originality.

If it becomes necessary for you to project your individual persona into the collective consciousness of the office environment, you may like to silently invoke and identify with a particular mythic archetype as a role model: Mercury for effective communications, Jupiter for skills in organisation and wise decision-making, Diana for intuition and Mars when assertiveness is required. You can also visualise a protective circle of power surrounding you as you interact with others, especially in your encounters with people whose power-based agendas are sounding warning bells. Practise focusing your sense of personal power in your solar plexus region (the upper part of the abdomen) and extending your circle of magical protection. This is also a good visualisation to use when you are going for a job interview, since one of the things a potential employer will be testing is your sense of self-esteem and personal worth. You are more likely to be respected if you project a sense of inner strength coupled with a powerful sense of personal boundaries.

The magic of trees, flowers and herbs

The world of Nature provides us with our spiritual sanctuary, whether we enjoy wandering in wilderness regions, exploring hills and mountains, resting beside lakes and meandering rivers or basking on sun-drenched beaches beside the ocean. However much we enjoy our work, it is always beneficial to get away from our regular routines and open ourselves to the enchantment and spontaneity of Nature. More likely than not it will be in the natural and unspoiled places within our environment that we find peace, deep inner sustenance and a true sense of tranquillity. It is through Nature that we connect directly to the spiritual vitality of life itself.

All cultures have recognised the uplifting and inspirational dimensions of the natural world, and so it is hardly surprising that many types of trees, flowers and herbs have been accorded special magical significance. Many of these symbolic meanings have passed into folklore, and these days some of these symbolic associations may seem quaint or even sentimental. However, they often evoke a type of lingering folk-memory which recalls the traditional paths of healing and enchantment. The symbolism of magical trees and plants can become part of our intuitive awakening if we include them within our rituals, meditations and visualisations.

Magical trees

Many trees have magical or symbolic associations. For example, the almond is said to promote abundance and prosperity, while the cedar symbolises good fortune and the cypress protection and long life. The hazel was a 'tree of wisdom' in Celtic mythology, and the birch a symbol of fertility. The chestnut is associated with prosperity and abundance, the myrtle with love and stable relationships, and the pine with friendship in the face of adversity. The fig tree is traditionally associated with wisdom and creativity, the quince with happiness, and the olive with peace (the ancient Greeks wore garlands of olive leaves in their hair as they prayed for an end to hostilities). Some trees have also been linked symbolically to specific months of the year, as well as to certain qualities and virtues:

* **January** Rowan – protection and success, psychic powers
* **February** Ash – prosperity and health
* **March** Alder – healing, the ability to control external forces
* **April** Willow – love, intuition and healing
* **May** Hawthorn – hope, fertility and happiness
* **June** Oak – strength, confidence, luck and financial success
* **July** Hazel – protection, good luck and wisdom
* **August** Apple – love and long life

* **September** Vine – strength, renewal and durability
* **October** Ivy – fidelity and longevity
* **November** Yew – death
* **December** Mistletoe – peace, protection, love, fertility and health

---

AN OAK TREE VISUALISATION

Locate an oak tree growing in a nearby vicinity. Choose a specimen that is tall and dignified, and take a few moments to reflect on the fact that, traditionally, this tree is regarded as 'the king of the woods'.

Stand barefoot beside the tree and reach out to touch it. Talk to it in a personal, loving way, and circle the tree three times in a clockwise direction. Now lean back against the tree with your palms resting flat against the trunk.

Close your eyes and begin to visualise the different stages of this noble tree's development. Visualise it first as a small acorn, then as a young sapling. Finally hold an image of this mature tree in your mind's eye, representing how it is today - with its leaves and branches reaching up to embrace the heavens.

Now imagine that your consciousness is merging with that of the tree itself. Feel yourself totally within it, so that its hard, scaly bark has become your skin and your arms have become its branches reaching up into the sky. Feel that your body and legs have become its trunk and that your feet have transformed into its roots, reaching deep down into the nourishing earth. Now visualise your life-blood and the sap of the tree becoming one, and experience this green energy flowing freely through your body, healing and regenerating you.

Once you feel that this spiritual union with the oak tree is complete and that the enriching fusion of energies has reached its peak, visualise the green energy of the oak slowly subsiding so that you once again begin to regain your individual identity and become distinct from the tree. Now you are ready to return to your own individual consciousness.

When you are ready, open your eyes, thank the tree for its healing qualities, and give a small blessing. If you wish, a small libation of honeymead, apple cider or beer can be poured over its roots by way of thanks.

Magical flowers and herbs

Like certain trees, many flowers and herbs also have magical significance. Some of these symbolic associations have arisen through the observation of the shape, texture, colour and perfume of different plants – the concept traditionally known as the 'doctrine of signatures' – while other associations have come down to us from classical mythology.

Among the best loved of all flowers, roses are universally associated with romantic love. Red roses are a symbol of passion, while pink roses are an expression of tenderness and white roses a symbol of purity. In Greek mythology the rose was sacred to Aphrodite, goddess of love, who pricked the soles of her feet on rose thorns while searching for her lover, Aries, god of war.

White lilies also have mythological associations and are regarded as a symbol of purity. According to Greek legend, white lilies are said to have sprung forth as milk spilled from Hera's breasts onto the earth. Lavender also has mythic connections. Sacred to Vesta, the Greek goddess of the hearth, lavender was used in love potions, and as a consequence lavender water has traditionally been sprinkled over the heads of young maidens to help preserve their chastity. Meanwhile, poppies, often associated with dreams, are said to have burst forth from the earth to help light Demeter's path as she searched in the darkness for her abducted daughter Persephone.

Some flowers, like morning glory, campanula, oxlip and cuckoo flower, are associated with the Virgin Mary and are also known as Goddess flowers, reflecting their pre-Christian associations; while other flowers, including primroses, red campion, periwinkles, cowslips and forget-me-nots, have a close connection with the fairies.

A FLOWER-SPIRIT MEDITATION

Sit in a comfortable place where you will not be disturbed. Go through a short relaxation and take a plant, fresh or dried, in your hands. Turn your attention inwards and onto the plant. Feel your psyche merging with that of the plant, gradually penetrating its essence.

Wait and a guide will come to you … If you feel good about her or him, then follow where she leads. Remember you can come back whenever you wish, and go as fast or as slow as you choose.[15]

Many flowers have more specific symbolic associations. Daisies, for example, are a symbol of innocence, violets are widely used as a comfort in times of sorrow, while tulips are associated with fame. Bluebells are associated symbolically with constancy, carnations with love, crocuses with happiness, chamomile with relaxation, cornflowers with fertility, cyclamens with confidence and inner strength, honeysuckle with devoted affection, hyacinths with playfulness, irises with faith, jasmine with romantic love and sexual passion, lilacs with purity, and snowdrops with hope.

Many herbs also have magical connotations. These include exotic and potentially dangerous plants like hemlock, henbane, deadly nightshade and thornapple, which were used in the so-called 'flying ointments' of medieval witches to produce aerial hallucinations and out-of-body trance states. However, other herbs have more mainstream associations.

One of the best known of all herbs, basil, came originally from India, where it was used as a remedy for snake bites and scorpion stings and was dedicated to the Hindu god Vishnu. In Italy and Lebanon, basil is regarded as a herb of courtship and is believed to attract lovers.

Coriander was regarded by the ancient Greeks as an aphrodisiac and was used in the preparation of love potions. Ginger is also traditionally regarded as an aphrodisiac and is said to arouse passion. Rosemary, on the other hand, is associated with fertility, and clusters of rosemary were brought to old Anglo-Saxon weddings for exactly this reason. However, Greek and Roman students in ancient times regarded this herb more as a stimulant for the mind, and they wore wreaths of rosemary around their heads in order to activate their memories and focus their thoughts.

For the purpose of magical visualisation, some of the symbolic associations between different plants, trees and herbs and the planetary rulers of classical mythology are provided in the chart on pages 116–17.

PLANTS AND THE PLANETARY RULERS
OF THE ZODIAC

	Flowers	*Herbs*	*Trees*
THE SUN rules *Leo*	Marigold, sunflower, buttercup, or any orange or golden flower	Cinnamon, rue, thyme	Laurel, palm, almond

Deities: Helios, Apollo, Sol

THE MOON rules *Cancer*	Gardenia, jasmine, or white flower	Lemon balm, moonwort	Willow, any mountain ash

Deities: Artemis, Selene, Hecate, Diana, Luna

MERCURY rules *Gemini*	Lavender, lily of the valley	Lemongrass, parsley	Almond, hazel
rules *Virgo*	Lavender, lily	Dill, fennel	Cypress, walnut

Deities: Hermes, Mercury

VENUS rules *Libra*	Primrose, hydrangea	Marjoram, vanilla	Olive
rules *Taurus*	Rose, lilac, violet	Thyme, vervain	Ash, apple

Deities: Aphrodite, Venus

	Flowers	*Herbs*	*Trees*
MARS rules *Aries*	Carnation, honeysuckle	Peppermint	Pine, holly
rules *Scorpio*	Poinsettia, geranium	Cumin, basil	Rowan, blackthorn

Deities: Aries, Mars

	Flowers	*Herbs*	*Trees*
JUPITER rules *Sagittarius*	Tulip, dandelion	Sage, feverfew	Oak, birch
rules *Pisces*	Water lily, sweet pea	Catnip	Alder, lemon

Deities: Zeus, Jupiter

	Flowers	*Herbs*	*Trees*
SATURN rules *Capricorn*	Pansy, magnolia	Comfrey	Yew, poplar
rules *Aquarius*	Orchid	Anise	Pear, cherry

Deities: Kronos, Saturn

CHAPTER FOUR

The magic of love and sexuality

Falling in love is surely one of the most wonderful things that can ever happen to us. When we are in love the whole world is an enchanted place; any boundaries between ourselves and the one we love dissolve, and we feel profoundly at one with each other. We share our lover's vitality and being, for we are intimately connected, and it is as if we have entered an entirely different, and quite remarkable, realm of awareness. Being in love transforms us completely. We experience the peaks of happiness in a much more intense and all-encompassing way than we have before. Every moment is magical, every moment is sublime, for love is one of the most uplifting experiences we can have in our everyday lives.

We all know that love and sexual intimacy are special, but is it also possible for love and sexual expression to become *sacred*? According to the magical wisdom traditions it is indeed possible. However, within the context of magical practice, if we are to transform love and sexuality so that they become truly sacred we have to move well beyond the physical and emotional dimensions of love and enter a spiritual domain. In this space we discover an innate divinity both within ourselves and also within our partner.

Obviously, this is a process which may take some time to evolve, and we may find that our own spiritual growth and that of our lover develop at different paces. However, a good way to begin is by exploring the many mythological expressions of love and sexual desire which have inspired lovers throughout the ages, and then seek to bring these sacred, mythic energies into our own lives. One of the most famous and inspirational archetypes of love, passion and beauty is provided to us by the Greek goddess Aphrodite.

Aphrodite – goddess of love

In ancient Greece, Aphrodite was the goddess of love, beauty and fertility. She was much admired for her lovely face and body, her spontaneous laughter, and her irresistible charm. Aphrodite had sanctuaries at Corinth, on the island of Cythera and at Eryx in western Sicily. Her cult seems to have come to Greece from Cyprus, where she was known as the goddess Kypris. Her Roman counterpart was the goddess Venus.

Different accounts of her birth have come down to us from classical myth and legend. According to Homer's *Iliad*, Aphrodite was the daughter of Zeus and the sea nymph Dione. However, Hesiod provides us with a different story in his *Theogony*. According to his account, Uranus, the tyrannical god of Heaven and Sky, had numerous offspring through his sexual union with Gaia, goddess of Earth. These offspring were the Titans, who personified the violent forces of Nature. Uranus imprisoned the Titans within the body of Gaia, but the burden of carrying these violent offspring soon became too overwhelming for her, so Kronos, the youngest son of Gaia, then rose up in revolt, castrated his father and threw his severed genitals into the sea. As soon as this happened, white foam gathered around the genitals, and then from the foam came forth a beautiful maiden. This was the goddess Aphrodite. The Greek word *aphros* means 'foam', which explains her name. The Renaissance artist Botticelli has depicted this remarkable scene in his famous painting *The Birth of Venus*.

In ancient Greece, Aphrodite was one of the twelve Olympians (gods and goddesses who lived on Mount Olympus) and she was especially celebrated for her frequent love affairs. Although married to the lame blacksmith Hephaestus, she had five children with the war god, Aries, and she also produced several offspring as a result of her sexual encounters with Hermes, Dionysus and Poseidon, as well as with a mortal, Anchises. Aphrodite later abandoned Mount Olympus because of her passionate love for Adonis, with whom she had a son and a daughter.

In spite of her numerous romances and sexual liaisons, the ancient Greeks made Aphrodite the divine patron of marriage. Also, because of the unique circumstances of her birth, she was regarded as a sea goddess, as well as a goddess of animals and gardens. In Greek mythology she is linked to the three Graces – the personifications of charm, grace and beauty – and also to the Horae, goddesses of the different seasons. Animals sacred to her include the dolphin, the ram, the swan, the dove and the sparrow. Her sacred flowers, trees and fruits include the rose, myrtle, cypress, pomegranate and golden apple.

In Roman mythology, Venus was a goddess not only of love, desire and beauty but also of friendship and partnership. As a planetary ruler she is associated with music and the arts, and in astrology she is regarded as a force for harmony, peace and reconciliation.

As a mythic figure, and as a prototype for sacred sexuality, Aphrodite has no peer. She calls us to open our hearts to passion and love, to ride the tides of emotion, to open ourselves to the joy of living, to surrender to the pleasure of the senses and to rejoice in the prospect of giving and receiving love. In this way Aphrodite is an inspiration to us all. Here is a prayer of devotion from a contemporary Wiccan priestess:

> Lady of Light and Love,
> help me to open my heart
> as the dawn breaks every day anew.
>
> Lady of Light and Love,
> help me to express passion
> as the noon sun blazes endlessly.
>
> Lady of Light and Love,
> help me to be compassionate
> as the evening shadows soften the world.
>
> Lady of Light and Love,
> help me to love wisely
> as the night brings endings and new beginnings.[1]

If, as part of your magical practice, you wish to create your own personal ritual to honour Aphrodite, you should incorporate as many features from her mythology as possible: her flowers, her plants, and images of her sacred animals. Symbolically she is associated with Friday ('Friday's child is loving and giving ...') and with the elements Water and Earth. Her traditional colours are green, indigo and rose-pink, her sacred metal is copper, her jewels are amber and emerald, and her incenses are benzoin, rose and jasmine.

Tantra and sacred sex

We must now turn briefly to the Indian mystical tradition to further our understanding of sacred sexuality. For many people, the expressions 'Tantra' and 'sexual yoga' are synonymous, but Tantra is much more than this. Its philosophies and practice are based on a very particular way of viewing the world and the ebb and flow of daily life. As we will see, the insights of the Tantric tradition have specific consequences for our understanding of everyday magic.

According to Tantric tradition, all aspects of creation reflect the dynamic flux and flow of opposing polarities, and this is expressed in the eternal Dance of Life – a never-ending dance between force and form. In our physical world of birth, life and death, new forms are forever coming into being as other forms dissolve. Within Tantric cosmology the goddess Shakti is the personification of energy and vitality while Lord Shiva represents containment and stability. Shakti herself is both a creator and a destroyer: on the one hand she epitomises all that is beautiful and pure, while on the other she also unleashes terror and destruction.

In Tantra the game of life is seen as an eternal love story in which all the dualities and opposing polarities of existence must finally be subsumed and resolved within a higher unity, for in the ultimate sense everything in the universe is essentially One. In the Tantric tradition this Oneness is symbolised by the sacred marriage of Shiva and Shakti.

Tantra also tells us something else – that the opposing forces of creation and destruction do not only engage with each other on an external level but also rage *within* each of us as well. The dynamic forces of the universe at large are *our own* inner forces too, for the gods and goddesses are mirrored in our consciousness. Their dance is our dance, their love can be our love. For this reason it is important that we regard Tantra not only as a tradition of sexual yoga but also as a form of mystical practice grounded in the philosophy of polar opposites. As Francis King has noted, 'All the opposites of which humanity is conscious can be resolved into a higher unity, the marriage of Shiva and Shakti … all existence is a by-product of the eternal loveplay between the polarities.'[2]

According to the Tantric teachings, all human beings have the goddess Shakti latent within them. The goddess takes the form of a serpent – Kundalini – which lies coiled and dormant at the base of the spine. However, the spiritual fire of the Kundalini serpent does not always have to remain dormant within us, for the power of Shakti can be awakened. The Shakti power can rise up through different energy centres in the body and give rise to new faculties of spiritual perception. And it can rise up in such a way that it finally produces a complete spiritual awakening, symbolised as the blossoming of the thousand-petalled lotus. In this way we begin to appreciate that in the Tantric tradition of Kundalini yoga, sexuality is regarded as an expression of divine energy. Tantra utilises sacred sexuality as a force for spiritual awakening.

Wiccan authority Carl Weschcke believes that Tantric philosophy has a direct bearing on Western magical practice, for in Tantra we are honouring the sacred vitality of the Universal Goddess:

> The essential message of Tantra is 'Look within – find, and express Divinity.' Learn to invoke God and Goddess within yourselves, learn to use the creative power of the Divinity within to transform Body and Soul, and to improve daily life ... Tantra knows that Sexual Energy is Feminine – it is the Goddess, the Mother, Holy Earth. All Life as we know it is of Her ... Every person, male and female both, is a 'channel' between God and Goddess – between Sky and Earth – and as we awaken to the Divinity within and open the channels for the ebb and flow of Divine Energies, we accelerate the evolution of consciousness, the healing of the Earth and all within Her ...[3]

Tantric practitioner Jonn Mumford confirms this: 'To see God/Goddess as incarnate in the person of your beloved, and to experience oneself as God/Goddess both in your inner essence as well as in the eyes of your lover is truly powerful magick!'[4]

Kundalini yoga and the chakras

As we have noted, in Kundalini yoga the latent Shakti energy at the base of the spine is awakened and raised through different energy centres in the body. According to the Tantric teachings there are seven of these major energy centres, or chakras, in the body. The first five are associated symbolically with the Tattva elements we described earlier (see pages 62–64).

The word 'yoga' itself comes from the Sanskrit word *yuj*, meaning 'to yoke', and the ultimate aim of yoga is spiritual union with the Higher Self, with the Godhead, with Brahman. In Kundalini yoga this union is expressed as the merging of two opposites – Shiva and Shakti – who, as we have seen, represent the male and female polarities of existence.

In Tantra, all manifestations of life-energy, intelligence, will, thoughts and feelings are regarded as feminine – as aspects of Shakti. As the Great Goddess she also encompasses the five elements Earth, Water, Fire, Air and Spirit from which the universe is formed. As Swami Sivananda Sarasvati has said of Shakti: 'She is the primal force of life that underlies all existence. She vitalises the body through her energy. She is the energy in the Sun, the fragrance in the flowers, the beauty in the landscape ... the whole world is her body.'5

Beyond the world of manifestation lies the transcendental domain of Lord Shiva. The sacred task of all devotees of Kundalini yoga is to awaken the energy of the Goddess – the Kundalini serpent energy – and ultimately to raise it to the highest chakra so she may once again be united with her lover in the supreme bliss of samadhi, the state of deep, meditative concentration.

Kundalini yoga clearly identifies this cosmic process as a sacred potential within every human being, for the gods and goddesses are within, and our task is to bring them to life and unleash their energy. There are numerous energy channels in the body – according to some yogic sources, as many as 350 000 – but the principal one in Kundalini yoga is the path which the Shakti energy should take in passing through the chakras to the crown of the head. This path is known as Sushumna (sometimes also spelled Shushumna), the energy channel, or *nadi*, which corresponds to the central nervous system of the body. Around Sushumna are coiled two other major channels – Pingala, which is masculine and associated with the heat of the Sun, and Ida, which is feminine and associated with the cool, reflected light of the Moon. According to the teachings of Kundalini yoga, Ida and Pingala meet in the lowest of the chakra energy centres, Muladhara, and also higher up in the sixth chakra, Ajna. The purpose of Kundalini yoga is to arouse the normally dormant energy of the serpent fire in Muladhara and then to raise the Shakti power through each of the chakras in turn, thereby lifting this sacred energy from the levels of physical sensory awareness through to the level of supreme spiritual Oneness in Sahasrara.

According to yoga authority Haridas Chaudhuri, some Western interpreters have identified the chakras too literally with specific nerve plexuses, ganglia and glands in the body. Chaudhuri describes the chakras as 'consciousness potentials', which only assume meaning as the Kundalini is aroused. The chakras themselves are said to lie within the Brahmanadi – the innermost channel within the Sushumna. And while there is a correlation between the chakras and various parts of the body, the chakras do not equate literally with them.[6] Nevertheless it is widely acknowledged that focusing one's awareness on these 'locations' is necessary for the purposes of visualisation.

Overleaf is a table of the seven chakras of Kundalini yoga, followed by a brief description of their symbolic associations.

THE SEVEN CHAKRAS OF KUNDALINI YOGA

First chakra: Muladhara (Earth)

Located at the base of the spine, near the coccyx and the anus, and associated with the pelvic plexuses, testes and ovaries. Muladhara is the location of the sleeping Kundalini serpent.

Second chakra: Svadisthana (Water)

Located just below the navel in the sacral region, and associated with the hypogastric plexus and adrenal glands. Svadisthana is associated with the genitals and sexuality, and symbolically with the menstrual cycle.

Third chakra: Manipura (Fire)

Located just above the navel in the lumbar region, and associated with the solar plexus, pancreas and liver. Manipura is associated symbolically with the fire of sexual passion.

Fourth chakra: Anahata (Air)

Located in the region of the heart, and associated with the cardiac plexus and thymus gland. Anahata is associated symbolically with love, compassion and the breath of new life.

Fifth chakra: Visuddha (Spirit)

Located near the Adam's apple in the throat, and associated with the pharyngeal plexus and thyroid gland.

Sixth chakra: Ajna

Located between the eyebrows, and associated with the nasociliary plexus and pituitary gland.

Seventh chakra: Sahasrara

Located on the crown of the head, and associated with the cerebrum and also with the pineal gland – which is sometimes referred to as the 'third eye'. Sahasrara is the sphere of supreme spiritual transcendence.

MULADHARA

The name of this chakra means 'root base' and it is both the foundation for personal growth and the gateway to the higher, more subtle spheres of spiritual awareness. This sphere represents not only the physical world but our total awareness of everyday reality. Muladhara is associated with the sense of smell.

SVADISTHANA

Literally Shakti's 'own abode', this chakra is the counterpart of the Jungian 'unconscious' and the 'astral planes' of occult tradition. It is also the centre of the basic sexual instincts and desires. Svadisthana is associated with the sense of taste.

MANIPURA

This chakra is known as 'the city [*pura*] of the lustrous gem [*mani*]' because of its connection with the element Fire. Regarded as the primal source of high ambition and personal power, it completes the triad of the three base chakras (the other two being Muladhara and Svadisthana) which govern the lives of most people in their everyday environment. However, Manipura represents the first light of the rising sun and therefore has within it the potential for higher spiritual vision. It is appropriately associated with the sense of sight.

ANAHATA

Regarded as the centre of unselfish love and spiritual values, this chakra is the heart centre. Anahata means 'unstruck sound' and it is in this sphere that, for the first time, the devotee hears the sound (*sabda*) of Brahman. In Anahata we learn to overcome our emotions, and the wind or breath of life, lifts us up to the higher spheres. Anahata is associated with the element Air, and also with the sense of touch.

VISUDDHA

From the Sanskrit word meaning 'completely purified', this chakra represents mastery of the four elements and the first encounter with Spirit. At the same time the devotee recognises that each individual life is a unique source of creative energy in the universe. In this sphere of awareness the inner world of Spirit is perceived as more real than the world of physical appearances. Visuddha is associated with the sense of hearing.

AJNA AND SAHASRARA

The two remaining chakras represent transcendental states of awareness and are essentially beyond the scope of visualisation and the creative imagination. For this reason, no specific visual symbols are ascribed to them. Ajna is known as the 'wisdom centre' and is associated with the mystical experience known in the West as 'cosmic consciousness'. In Ajna the complementary energy channels Ida and Pingala meet for the first time after emerging from the base chakra, Muladhara. In the Kundalini yoga tradition the ruling deity of this sphere is androgynous – a combination of Shiva and Shakti. However, in the higher sphere of Sahasrara duality is transcended altogether. Here the union of Shakti and Shiva dissolves all manifested forms and there is only the Oneness of Brahman. Sahasrara is the doorway to the Void of formlessness (*sunya*).

The Middle Pillar Exercise

Having made a detour into the realm of Tantra and its exploration of sexual polarities, we can now return to the Kabbalah which, through its symbol of the Tree of Life, provides us with a framework for exploring different levels of magical consciousness.

We have already seen that the Kabbalists have always regarded the Tree of Life not only as a composite symbol of the process of divine Creation but also as a symbolic matrix encompassing the spiritual energy centres within every human being. When the sephiroth, or spiritual energy centres, of the Tree of Life are superimposed upon the human body, they align themselves in three vertical pillars. The central pillar forms an axis with its peak in Kether, the Crown – an energy centre associated with the crown of the head. The base of the pillar is in Malkuth, the Kingdom, which represents Earth and is associated with the feet. The outer pillars align vertically with the shoulders and arms.

Four of the ten sephiroth may be found on the central axis: Kether, Tiphareth, Yesod and Malkuth. However, in the space between Kether and Tiphareth we often find reference to another sphere known as Daath (Knowledge), a spiritual centre which marks the divide between the sacred, transcendent energies of the Trinity (Kether–Chokmah–Binah) and the seven spheres, or 'days', of Creation further down. Daath is the invisible eleventh sephirah but it is not usually included on the Tree because in Jewish tradition ten (consisting of three plus seven) was regarded as a spiritual number, whereas eleven does not have the same sacred symmetry.

The spiritual spheres on the central axis of the Tree of Life, and the energy paths which connect them, are known collectively as the Middle Pillar. As one would perhaps expect, the so-called Middle Pillar Exercise, a visionary meditation in Western magic involving the passage of spiritual energy, correlates to some extent with the chakra system in Tantra. However, there is one important difference, as Francis King points out:

> The Middle Pillar Exercise is a sort of Kundalini Yoga in reverse. In the latter the serpent power is awakened from its sleep at the base of the spine, i.e. the Muladhara chakra, and rises through, successively, the Svadisthana, Manipura, Anahata, Vishuddha and Ajna chakras until, finally, it reaches the Sahasrara chakra where the Shiva/Shakti marriage takes place.
>
> In the Middle Pillar Exercise the energy flow is downwards from the Sahasrara chakra (Kether) to the Ajna and Vishudda chakras (Daath as the focus of Chokmah and Binah), to the Manipura and Anahata chakras (Tiphareth), to the Svadisthana chakra (Yesod as the focus of the astral triangle) and to the Muladhara chakra (Yesod proper). Finally the energy flow is earthed in Malkuth.[7]

As Francis King indicates, the magician who wishes to achieve the marriage of Shiva and Shakti within the context of the Western magical tradition would have to perform the Middle Pillar Exercise in reverse, but this is more than simply a matter of directing energy. It becomes a task of 'marrying' Malkuth and Yesod with 'the Divine White Brilliance of Kether' in the sacred union of essence and form.

Here is a table which shows the correlations between the Tantric chakras and the sephiroth on the Middle Pillar of the Tree of Life. As before, we proceed from the lowest level of the base chakra (Malkuth/Muladhara) through to the highest (Kether/Sahasrara). However, the colours for vibrating the different spheres on the Middle Pillar differ from those ascribed to the Tattvas, and in my view it is better not to mix them. Tantra is an Eastern system and the Kabbalah is a Western system, and for the purposes of magical visualisation we have to regard them as parallel but separate.

THE KUNDALINI CHAKRAS AND THE SPHERES ON THE KABBALISTIC TREE OF LIFE

Sephirah	Chakra	Tattva	Tattva symbol
Malkuth (colour: very dark green or black)	*Muladhara*	*Earth*	*Yellow square*
Yesod (colour: purple tinged with silver)	*Svadisthana*	*Water*	*Silver crescent*
Tiphareth (colour: golden yellow)	*Manipura*	*Fire*	*Red triangle*
Tiphareth (colour: golden yellow)	*Anahata*	*Air*	*Blue circle*
Daath (colour: violet tinged with blue)	*Vishuddha*	*Spirit*	*Black oval*
—	*Ajna*	—	*(no image)*
Kether (colour: pure white)	*Sahasrara*	—	*(no image)*

Note: Manipura and Anahata both correlate with Tiphareth in this table. Some Tantric practitioners also maintain that Muladhara is really a combination of Malkuth and Yesod because in yogic cross-legged meditation postures the coccyx provides one's basic contact with the earth, rather than the feet.

In Chapter Three we described the procedure for the Kabbalistic Cross and the Banishing Ritual of the Pentagram (see pages 94–97). The Middle Pillar Exercise commences with these two visualisations, because the first activity in any magical ritual is always to establish the sacred space – the magic circle – and then to activate the spiritual energies within our own sphere of consciousness. In the Middle Pillar visualisation itself we will be drawing the sacred energy of *Ain Soph Aur* – the Infinite Light – down through the crown of the head. Then we will draw it down still further so it descends, sphere by sphere, through each of the energy centres in the body.

The Middle Pillar visualisation

Having performed the Kabbalistic Cross and the Banishing Ritual of the Pentagram, face towards the east and imagine a sphere of vibrant pure white light radiating just above the crown of your head. After you have succeeded in focusing your awareness on this sphere of light, draw it down into the crown of your head and vibrate the god-name 'AHIH' (pronounced 'Eeh-hee-yay'). This is the visualisation for the sphere of Kether.

Now draw this light down through the central axis of your body so that it reaches your throat. Visualise this energy centre as a sphere of vibrant blue/violet light and vibrate the god-name 'YHVH ELOHIM' (pronounced 'Ye-ho-waah El-oh-heem'). This is the visualisation for the sphere of Daath.

Bring the light down from your throat to the region of your solar plexus. Visualise this energy centre as a sphere of vibrant golden yellow light and vibrate the god-name 'YHVH ELOAH VA DAAT' (pronounced 'Ye-ho-waah El-oh-ah Va Da-art'). This is the visualisation for the sphere of Tiphareth.

Now draw the light down into the regions of your genitals. Visualise this energy centre as a sphere of vibrant purple/silver light and vibrate the god-name 'SHADDAI EL CHAI' (pronounced 'Shah-dai El Haii'). This is the visualisation for the sphere of Yesod.

Finally, bring the light down to the soles of your feet and imagine that it is spreading out beneath your feet to form a perfect circle. Traditionally this sphere is associated with a grouping of Earth colours – russet, olive, citrine and black. If you find it difficult visualising this cluster of colours, visualise the sphere as very dark green or black and vibrate the god-name 'ADNI HA ARETZ' (pronounced 'Aah-doh-naii Haa Ah-retz'). This is the visualisation for the sphere of Malkuth.

Later, when you have become proficient in this visualisation – which of course focuses on drawing the sacred light *downwards* – you can extend the Middle Pillar Exercise by then raising the spiritual light up from Malkuth and returning it, sphere by sphere, to its sacred source beyond Kether. It is said in the Kabbalah that *Ain Soph Aur* is the Bridegroom of Shekinah and that Shekinah is the Bride or Queen who resides in Malkuth. In the Kabbalah, Shekinah is the equivalent of the Universal Goddess: she is the feminine face of God. Her home is in the sphere of Malkuth, symbolised by the element Earth: a centre of feminine energy. By raising the sacred light from Malkuth and bringing it back to Kether and beyond, we are performing the Kabbalistic equivalent of the sacred marriage of Shakti and Shiva. This results finally in a state of Divine Union – the transcendent and blissful attainment of Oneness.

We will return to this theme later, for on this level we are dealing with the sacred union of the Goddess and the God. For the moment, however, we are operating purely on the level of everyday magic – the magic of two loving partners who wish to express their love and sexuality within the context of sacred ritual.

Loving your body

Your journey into sacred sex is about to begin. Your partner can be an opposite-sex or same-sex partner – the magic works just the same. However, we have to remember that in the expression of sexual energy we are dealing with polar opposites, and in the case of a heterosexual couple this distinction is easier to make. With same-sex couples working magically, one partner will have to consciously embody the active sexual current of the Sun, and the other partner the receptive current of the Moon.

Sacred sex should always be based on mutual trust and equality, because both partners must feel they are fully engaging with each other on all levels of sensory awareness: physically, emotionally, intellectually and spiritually. There may be some forms of sexual intimacy that you or your partner are uncomfortable with – for example, some people don't like to be touched or stroked excessively, while others don't enjoy oral sex – so you will have to decide beforehand if there are any restrictions in your lovemaking.

Having established the basis for your shared sexual expression, the important thing to remember about magical sex is that it allows you to rediscover the peaks of passion and sensory pleasure. However, this involves feeling good about your body in the first instance. To explore how you feel about who you really are, you may find it helpful to make some affirmations about your own naked body. You can start by making these affirmations to yourself, naked, in front of a full-length mirror. Tackle this exercise at a time when you feel good about yourself. Turn the lights down or use candles.

Loving your body as it is

Say to your feet:

> *I love you. You provide my support in the world and my contact with the earth.*

Say to your legs and buttocks:

> *I love you. You are my strength in the world,*
> *and my movement.*

Say to your genitals:

> *I love you. You provide my pleasure and the*
> *power of sexuality.*

Say to your stomach:

> *I love you. You absorb my food and nourish my physical*
> *being, and give away what I do not need.*

Say to your chest and lungs:

> *I love you. You take in air and purify my blood.*

Say to your arms and hands:

I love you. You perform my work and allow me to act in the world.

Say to your back:

I love you. You keep me upright and support all the movements I make.

Say to your neck:

I love you. You house the voice which allows me to communicate to the world.

Say to your head:

I love you. You take in food and air and all my knowledge of the world. [8]

A temple of love

This is just the beginning. Now that you have accepted your physical body, perfect or imperfect as it may be, the next step is to visualise your body as a temple of sacred spirituality, as a sacred space for the manifestation of divine energy. It is through your body that you will express your sense of the sacred, and through your body that you will invoke the Goddess or the God.

As we discussed earlier, Tantra is all about activating the sacred energies which lead to spiritual awakening, and this is also true of magical sexuality. As one practitioner has observed: 'Sexuality is not just about the physical body but also about the energy body ... Sexuality alters the flow of that energy in profound ways. Consciously understanding that process, accepting it, and controlling it, turns sex into magic.'9

It is easier to think of our body as a temple if we approach it with reverence. Rather than relating to the body purely in physical terms, we can consciously regard it more imaginatively, and more sensitively, by evoking the language of myth and metaphor. This might involve, for example, referring to the vulva as a flower or sacred altar, to the nipples as little gemstones or sweet, soft fruit, or to the clitoris as a pearl in an oyster. The penis might become a spire or sacred wand, while you can think of semen as the elixir of life, and body fluids generally as honey, ambrosia or nectar. This brings some of the magic back into sex immediately, and will help you regard all aspects of your sexual expression as sacred.

Before you begin your sacred lovemaking you should psychically cleanse and purify your ritual space in ways we have already described. Make sure you are feeling pleasantly relaxed to begin with; soft candlelight and luxurious, sensuous rose or jasmine incense will certainly help establish a suitable ambience. Then you might wish to begin by looking deeply into each other's eyes and follow this by sensitively exploring the soft textures and subtle undulations of each other's body. This may also be a nice time to make a pledge of mutual caring and respect to your partner: 'Your pleasure is my pleasure. Pleasure is in touch. I love to touch you. My body is sacred. Your body is sacred.' In time you will come to regard your sexual expression as a play of divine energy which manifests on both a spiritual and physical level, and you will also bring a new feeling of reverence to your relationship with your partner.

Now, as your lovemaking begins, use your knowledge of either the Kundalini chakras or the sephiroth of the Middle Pillar to visualise a stream of vibrant light uniting all the energy centres in your body. Visualise the appropriate colours pulsing with all the vibrancy you can summon in your mind's eye, and imagine the stream of radiant white light building in intensity and coursing through your body like a current of electricity – up from your genital region to the crown of your head, and then down through your mouth and chest to your genitals once again. Encourage your partner to do the same and then, as your bodies fold into each other, bring your crown chakra centres together so that they touch and bond in an exchange of magical energy. You may also be able to visualise a single stream of magical light coursing up your spine from your genital region and then moving from your own forehead across to that of your partner. Your partner can then draw this energy down through their spinal column to their own genital region and transmit it back to you, completing the energy circuit. Try moving this circle of light energy in the reverse direction to see if this makes the flow of energy warmer (Sun current) or cooler (Moon current), and to see whether any strong mythological or magical images arise into your conscious awareness during your lovemaking.

As the energy of your mutual passion builds towards a climax, you will surely feel the sweet bliss of spiritual union sweeping through you, and now – as you feel uplifted on a wave of ecstasy – your personal boundaries will begin to dissolve. This type of lovemaking is really a type of worship, and the pleasure you experience in this magical context is not the pleasure of self-gratification or hedonistic sensuality but a spiritual offering in itself. Engage with that complete sense of self-surrender which comes with ecstatic release, and at the moment of climax dedicate your pleasure through your crown chakra to a special God or Goddess, or to the transcendent Spirit of Life itself.

According to Tantric tradition, whatever is held in the imagination at the moment of orgasm will come to pass, so make sure that this special moment is dedicated to a sacred purpose, for this then opens your conscious awareness to the possibility of personal spiritual transformation. Maybe at this time the God or Goddess will speak to you in a special and intimate manner, or you will be filled with Spirit in ways beyond your normal comprehension.

After your lovemaking you may wish to give thanks to the God or Goddess for any blessings you have received, and also spend some time relaxing and sharing what you have experienced with your lover. Whatever the outcome, you can be assured that if your sacred lovemaking is conceived as an invocation to a Goddess or a God, you will have dedicated your body, and your ecstatic pleasure, to the noblest cause of all – a celebration of the Divine.

Sacred union

Perhaps during your sacred lovemaking you sought to incarnate the love and sensual passion of the goddess Aphrodite, while your partner embodied the sensitivity and beauty of Aphrodite's favourite lover, Adonis. You can, in fact, choose any pairing of deities that you desire during your lovemaking, for all gods and goddesses are an expression of the Divine, and invoking and embodying their qualities within your own being raises your own expression of sexual love to the level of spiritual ecstasy.

In several mystical traditions, sacred sexual union is recognised as a symbol of spiritual transcendence. We have already seen that in the Kabbalah, *Ain Soph Aur* – the 'Infinite Light of the Innermost Being of God' – is regarded as the Bridegroom of Shekinah – the Bride or Queen who resides in Malkuth at the foot of the Tree of Life – and the task of the mystic is to invoke the spiritual potency of Shekinah and unite her in sacred marriage with the Godhead.

In Tantra the sacred marriage of Shakti and Shiva takes place in a blissful, transcendent state of consciousness where duality, or the division of sexual polarities, no longer exists. Similarly, during the third and final initiation in Wicca, the Great Rite climaxes with the sacred sexual union of the High Priestess and the High Priest. In this ritual the High Priestess and High Priest invoke the God and Goddess into each other so that their union is not one of two individual lovers but of God and Goddess cojoined as One. Their sexual union takes place simultaneously on both a physical and spiritual level, and their sexual congress becomes a sacred act, symbolic of Creation and the universal life-force itself.

In spiritual alchemy – the alchemy of personal transformation – the bonding of sacred lovers is symbolised by the sacred marriage of the Red Lion and the White Eagle, who represent the Sun and Moon respectively. The Red Lion is associated with the elements Fire and Air and the White Eagle with Earth and Water, and from their sacred marriage the Philosopher's Stone is born. In alchemy the Philosopher's Stone is a symbol of perfection because, according to alchemical tradition, it is this Stone which transforms the base metal lead into gold. In some alchemical accounts it is said that the Red Lion and the White Eagle unite and then die and putrefy, their death as individual King and Queen resulting in the subsequent release of Spirit. This is an alchemical metaphor for the bonding of sexual opposites which in turn results in the 'death' of the distinction between male and female and the 'birth' of the Spirit, for ultimate transcendence is a state of Oneness in which there are no polar opposites.

One of the mystical symbols for this state of Divine Unity is that of the sacred androgyne, represented by the image of the King and Queen joined together in a single body. The central idea behind an image like this is that of the sacred bonding of opposite sexual polarities, which then leads to ecstatic transcendence. Similarly, in the Kabbalah the sphere of Kether at the very peak of the Tree of Life is regarded as a state of spiritual consciousness which is neither male nor female – a state of Unity which transcends both sexual polarities.

This transcendence of sexual polarities is precisely what happens during sacred sex, for here we experience a similar dissolution of personal boundaries and the loss of our own sense of individual separateness. Many of us have experienced this dissolution of personal boundaries at the moment of sexual orgasm. For some people a climax like this becomes a spiritual peak-experience, a state of transcendent ecstasy. From a magical perspective we can say that, at special moments like this, the sacred union of the Sun and Moon – the God and Goddess – becomes a true celebration of the Oneness of the Divine.

CHAPTER FIVE

Visionary magic — a journey
of self-discovery

I have always been fascinated by the visionary aspect of magic because, for me, this type of magic leads directly to the potentials of greater self-awareness. Visionary magic shows us a way of exploring the archetypal forces of the creative imagination — energies and images which have inspired art, music and cosmology throughout the ages.

Visionary magic also offers us a path to spiritual self-transformation. As we have seen, all forms of magic are really a way of manifesting our hopes and aspirations — our personal vision for ourselves and the world we live in. And if our vision is large enough, our magic can open our awareness to a universe rich with possibility and diversity. I quoted Dr John Lilly earlier in this book, and his advice is worth repeating: 'In the province of the mind, what is believed to be true is true, or becomes true ... In the province of the mind, there are no limits.'[1]

Magic offers us many pathways to expanded awareness. These include magical ritual, the 'assumption of the God-form' and the path of sacred sexuality, which we have just explored. But there are other visionary approaches as well, and in all of these we will similarly make use of our magical will and our powers of creative visualisation. At this point we can explore three further types of visionary magic:

* The Tattvas – visionary magic of the five elements
* The Major Arcana – visionary magic of the Tarot
* Shamanism – visionary magic and the journey of the soul

The visionary magic of the Tattvas

Earlier we described the five Tattvas – the Hindu elements Earth, Water, Fire, Air and Spirit – which are associated with the first five chakras in Kundalini yoga. We mentioned too that they have been incorporated into the Western magical tradition. A study of the Tattvas was required of all magicians entering the Hermetic Order of the Golden Dawn – arguably the most influential magical organisation in the history of Western magic – and here the Tattvas were used as doorways to the magical imagination. For these magicians the Tattvas became a means of exploring visionary consciousness.

Here, to remind you, are the symbolic forms of the five Tattvas again:

* *Prithivi*, a yellow square, representing the element Earth

* *Apas*, a horizontal silver crescent with its tips facing upwards, representing the element Water
* *Vayu*, a blue circle, representing the element Air
* *Tejas*, a red triangle, representing the element Fire
* *Akasha*, a black oval, representing Spirit

Just over a hundred years ago the magicians of the Golden Dawn developed a technique for using the Tattvas as doorways to the visionary imagination. Here is a description of the technique they employed, written by Moina Mathers, wife of one of the founders of the Golden Dawn. In this account the variant spelling 'tattwa' is used, and Mrs Mathers is referring in the first instance to a composite image which combines the Tattva symbols for Earth and Water:

> Supposing the symbol you were experimenting with was Prithivi of Apas, that is, the 'earthly aspect of elemental Water', represented by a miniature yellow square mounted on a silver crescent, then fill your mind with the ideas thus symbolised. Place the tattwa card before you ... and look at the symbol long and steadily until you can perceive it clearly as a thought vision when you shut your eyes ... It may help you to perceive it as a large crescent made of blue or silvery water containing a cube of yellow sand. Continue trying to acquire a keen perception of the tattwa until ... its shape and its qualities shall seem to have become a part of you, and you should then begin to feel as though you were one with that particular Element, i.e. the main Element of your tattwa – in this case, Apas, elemental Water, completely bathed in it, and as if all other Elements were non-existent. If this be correctly done, you will find that the thought of any other Element

than the one with which you are working will be distinctly distasteful to you.

Having succeeded in obtaining the thought vision of the symbol, continue ... with the idea well fixed in your mind of calling before you on the card a brain picture of some scene or landscape. This, when it first appears, will probably be vague, but continue to 'make it more real', of whatever nature – deriving from perhaps imagination or memory – you believe it to be. Imagination and memory being analogous to the faculty that you are employing, the probability of their arising at this early stage will be great ... The thought picture may eventually become so clear to you (although this may be a matter of time and much practice) that it will seem as though the picture were trying to precipitate through the symbol ... the picture will be as nearly clear to the perception as a material one might be. But you can arrive at a great deal by merely receiving the impression of the landscape as a thought.

[Follow] the rules given ... until the point where the symbol of the tattwa has become perfectly vivid to the perception and when you feel as though you were almost one with the Element. You may modify the earlier stages of the working by so enlarging the symbol astrally, i.e. by the use of the visual imagination [so] that a human being can pass through it. When very vivid, and not until then, pass, spring or fly through it ... till you find yourself in some place or landscape ... It would appear well to act exactly as one would in a physical experience of a landscape, realising each step as one goes, not trying to look on both sides at once, or at the back of one's head, but turning first to the right hand and examining that, then turning to the left, then right around, and so on ... The more practically the experiences are worked, the more chance of success.[2]

These instructions for using the Tattvas, first written down in 1897, refer to 'brain pictures', 'thought visions' and 'thought pictures' – techniques we would today refer to as 'creative visualisation' or 'magical imaging'. But regardless of terminology, the techniques themselves have always proved very effective. Moina Mathers and her colleagues in the Golden Dawn soon found that they could use their Tattva visualisations to enter new realms of magical awareness.

Golden Dawn *Flying Roll XI*, a document which dates from 1893, describes a Tattva vision by Moina Mathers as she sat meditating in her ceremonial robes, contemplating a Tattva card combining *Tejas* and *Akasha* – a black egg within a red triangle (Spirit within Fire). The symbol seemed to grow before her gaze, enabling her to pass into a 'vast triangle of flame'. She then felt herself to be in a harsh, sandy desert. Intoning the god-name *Elohim*, she perceived a small pyramid in the distance and, drawing closer, she then noticed a small door on each face. She then vibrated the magical name *Sephariel* and a warrior appeared, leading a procession of guards. After a series of tests involving ritual grade signs, the guards knelt before her and she passed inside:

> ... dazzling light, as in a Temple. An altar in the midst – kneeling figures surround it, there is a dais beyond, and many figures upon it – they seem to be Elementals of a fiery nature ... She sees a pentagram, puts a Leo in it [a Fire sign], thanks the figure who conducts her – wills to pass through the pyramid, finds herself out amid the

sand. Wills her return – returns – perceiving her body in robes.[3]

We can see from this account that the visionary landscape Moina Mathers entered was closely related to the meditation symbol for Fire. The intangible aspect of the vision – represented by *Akasha*, or Spirit – seems to be reflected in the image of the sacred pyramid, which in this case she was able to 'enter' in her magical vision. The strange beings she perceived during her visionary encounter – fire elementals, or personifications of the element Fire – are creatures usually associated with the imagery of alchemy.

On another occasion Moina Mathers was able to invoke magical beings of a more cosmic or archetypal nature. Here she made use of the Tattva combination for Water and Spirit, and once again her account shows a direct connection between the magical symbol and the visionary beings who appeared:

A wide expanse of water with many reflections of bright light [were visible], and occasionally glimpses of rainbow colours appearing. When divine and other names were pronounced, elementals of the mermaid and merman type [would] appear, but few of the other elemental forms. These water forms were extremely changeable, one moment appearing as solid mermaids and mermen, the next melting into foam.

Raising myself by means of the highest symbols I had been taught, and vibrating the names of Water, I rose until the Water vanished, and instead I beheld a mighty world or globe, with its dimensions and divisions of Gods, Angels, elementals and demons – the whole Universe of Water. I called on HCOMA and there appeared standing before me a mighty Archangel, with four wings, robed in glistening white and crowned. In one hand, the right, he held a species of trident, and in the left a Cup filled to the brim with an essence which he poured down below on either side.[4]

In this vision Moina Mathers was able to use her knowledge of magical god-names to invoke powerful spirit guides, with the result that an archangel appeared to her during her exploration of the visionary landscape.

From a magical perspective it is clear that Tattvas are both powerful and direct, and they are undoubtedly very useful to help us explore the visionary dimensions of the elements Earth, Water, Fire, Air and Spirit. However, some magicians believe – and I agree with this view myself – that the Tattvas are comparatively restricted in their application because they tend to confine the visionary encounter to the specific symbol which the meditator has selected. There has always been a need for visionary encounters to be, in a sense, open-ended. They have to offer the possibility for personal growth, exploration and transcendence.

So within the field of visionary magic a more complete exploration of magical consciousness would obviously require a more extensive range of meditative symbols. The Golden Dawn magicians discovered that an ideal range of magical symbols could be found in the Tarot, and specifically in the Major Arcana, or mythic cards, of the Tarot deck.

Revisiting the Kabbalah and the Tarot

As mentioned earlier, it was the French ceremonial magician Eliphas Levi who first suggested locating the Major Arcana of the Tarot as symbolic pathways on the Kabbalistic symbol of the Tree of Life. Levi influenced several of the magicians in the Golden Dawn, and when Moina Mathers and her colleagues experimented with Tarot card visualisations they discovered that they were even more powerful than their Tattva visions.

A Golden Dawn trance vision recorded in November 1892 by Florence Farr and Elaine Simpson survives in a document known as *Flying Roll IV*. It is particularly interesting because it indicates the visionary magician's direct encounter with the gods and goddesses of the Tree of Life. A blend of Christian and Egyptian elements is also present – the Grail Mother is regarded here as an aspect of the Egyptian goddess Isis – and a ritual gesture appropriate to the Roman goddess Venus is also included. The Golden Dawn magicians were intrigued by the overlapping symbolism, or 'magical correspondences', of the various gods and goddesses from different mythologies and religions.

The Tarot Trump *The Empress* was taken; placed before the persons and contemplated upon, spiritualised, heightened in colouring, purified in design and idealised.

In vibratory manner, pronounced *Daleth*. Then, in spirit, saw a greenish blue distant landscape, suggestive of medieval tapestry. Effort to ascend was then made; rising on the planes; seemed to pass up through clouds and then appeared a pale green landscape and in its midst a Gothic Temple of ghostly outlines marked with light.

Approached it and found the temple gained in definiteness and was concrete, and seemed a solid structure. Giving the signs of the Netzach Grade (because of Venus) was able to enter; giving also Portal signs and 5=6 signs in thought form.[5] Opposite the entrance perceived a cross with three bars and a dove upon it; and beside this were steps leading downwards into the dark, by a dark passage. Here was met a beautiful green dragon, who moved aside, meaning no harm, and the spirit vision passed on. Turning a corner and still passing on in the dark emerged from the darkness onto a marble terrace brilliantly white, and a garden beyond, with flowers, whose foliage was of a delicate green kind and the leaves seemed to have a white velvety surface beneath. Here there appeared a woman of heroic proportions, clothed in green with a jewelled girdle, a crown of stars on her head, in her hand a sceptre of gold, having at one apex a lustrously white closed lotus flower; in her left hand an orb bearing a cross.

She smiled proudly, and as the human spirit sought her name, replied:

I am the mighty Mother Isis; the most powerful of all the world, I am she who fights not, but is always victorious, I am that Sleeping Beauty who men have sought, for all time; and the paths which lead to my castle are beset with dangers and illusions. Such as fail to find me sleep – or may ever rush after the Fata Morgana leading astray all who feel that illusory influence – I am lifted up on high and do draw men unto me. I am the world's desire, but few there be who find me. When my secret is told, it is the secret of the Holy Grail .

Asking to learn it, [she] replied:

Come with me, but first clothe in white garments, put on your insignia, and with bared feet follow where I shall lead.

Arriving at length at a Marble Wall, pressed a secret spring and entered a small compartment where the spirit seemed to ascend through a dense vapour, and emerged upon a turret of a building. Perceived some object in the midst of the place, but was forbidden to look at it until permission was accorded. Stretched out the arms and bowed the head to the Sun which was rising a golden orb in the East. Then turning, knelt with the face towards the centre, and being permitted to raise the eyes beheld a cup with a heart and the sun shining upon these; there seemed a clear ruby-coloured fluid in the cup. Then 'Lady Venus' said:

This is love, I have plucked out my heart and have given it to the world; that is my strength. Love is the mother of the Man-God , giving the Quintessence of her life to save mankind from destruction and to show forth the path to life eternal. Love is the mother of Christ ...
Spirit, and this Christ is the highest love – Christ is the heart of love, the heart of the Great Mother Isis – the Isis of Nature. He is the expression of her power – she is the Holy Grail, and He is the life blood of spirit, that is found in this cup.

After this, being told that man's hope lay in following her example, we solemnly gave our hearts to the keeping of the Grail; then, instead of feeling death, as our human imagination led us to expect, we felt an influx of the highest courage and power, for our own hearts were to be henceforth in touch with hers – the strongest force in all the world.
So then we went away, feeling glad that we had learned that 'He who gives away his life, will gain it.' For *that* love which is power, is given unto him – who hath given away his all for the good of others.[6]

As we can see from this fascinating trance account, the blend of magical imagery explored in the Golden Dawn resulted in an unusual visionary mix. This particular episode contained ancient Egyptian, Christian and Celtic elements, and from the viewpoint of the Golden Dawn magicians these particular mythologies were all regarded as part of a universal spiritual perspective.

Creating your own Tarot pathworkings

As we saw earlier, the 22 Tarot cards of the Major Arcana can be mapped as mythic pathways linking the ten different spheres of the Kabbalistic Tree of Life (see pages 20–30). Focusing on specific Tarot images and using them as visionary doorways to higher levels of magical awareness involves visualisations known as 'pathworkings'. Depending on which part of the Tree of Life you have chosen for your journey into the mythic inner world, you can plot your path from sphere to sphere and select the particular Tarot paths you wish to explore. You will then enter these paths through your powers of magical visualisation.

At this point you may wish to refer back to the first chapter of this book which includes a summary of the basic imagery associated with each of the cards in the Major Arcana (see pages 22–30). You may also find it useful to research the symbolism of individual cards in specialist books on the Tarot (see Bibliography). After you have assembled details of all the pertinent imagery, prepare your own description of the Tarot path you have selected. Make your description as 'visual' as you can, then make a tape-recording of your description or ask a friend to read aloud to you while you are relaxing and concentrating on the Tarot card you have chosen so that the Tarot card becomes the focus of your visualisation. This will allow you to make the visionary journey in your magical imagination.

Here are some examples of how your Tarot visualisations, or 'pathworkings', might read. Remember to keep them in the present tense.

THE WORLD

Tides of energy flow all around me as I find myself in the presence of the sacred Maiden of the Earth. Her pure face is filled with sunlight - light which nourishes the leaves and flowers in the deep,.abundant valley - and her flowing hair is the colour of golden wheat. The sacred maiden dances naked upon the grass and a soft light plays upon her fair skin ...

Persephone is like a beacon. Through her every movement I feel a sense of enrichment and warmth, and her radiant hair glistens like the newly risen sun casting its light across the fields.

But now in her eyes I see reflections of the Moon, and the sacred maiden says she will now lead me into the twilight world beneath the earth and beyond the sky, where her dark sister rules the land of shadows ...

And so now the sacred maiden prepares to take me on the first path of my sacred journey. She leads me through a passage in the earth towards a world beyond time.

THE STAR

In the night sky a golden star glows with crystal light and I see a beautiful naked maiden standing in a fast-flowing stream. Now I notice that she is holding a flask aloft so that it is open to the heavens above. I see that she is capturing life-essence with this flask – life-essence which now flows down from the golden star above. Shimmering light flows through her body, and she herself has become like a translucent vessel as she pours the waters of life into a pool below.

Suddenly I see that as these waters overflow upon the surrounding earth, everything around me now springs to life and offers new hope and possibility. The star-maiden tells me that I too can learn to transmit the light, and that new hope and abundance will then flow through me in turn.

THE EMPEROR

Amidst the textured rocks of the timeless mountains which now present themselves before me, I come before the throned ruler of the Universe. He is awesome and all-knowing, merciful and just. His crown shines with pure light, and his cloak is fashioned from the fabric of the Universe. He looks out upon all the living beings and creatures of the world, presiding over life in all its many forms and manifestations. His throne and surroundings are illumined by a reddish glow – the warm sun of Sacred Knowledge.

And still the Emperor sits in silent vigil, ever-patient upon his throne. From his supreme vantage point high up in the heavens he looks out, ever watchful, protective of all those in his care. He shows me now that all aspects of Creation are subject to flux and change, that life flows through death into life again in an ageless cycle that is without beginning and end. Through all these aeons he is with me, guiding my passage upon the Tree of Life.

How one chooses to present the material for Tarot path-workings is of course very much a matter of individual preference. The important thing is that each pathway in turn should come alive in your mind's eye as you prepare to proceed on your inner journey. It is also a good idea to prepare the written text for each pathworking in such a way that it is open-ended. In this way you do not anticipate what you may learn on each Tarot path, and you leave open the possibility that the gods and goddesses of the Tree of Life will share their wisdom and knowledge with you. It is also useful to keep a diary of your Tarot pathworkings so you can reflect later upon what has been given to you during your spiritual quest. A complete mystical journey of the Major Arcana is described in *The Book of Visions*, which is included as a supplementary text at the back of this book. You may find some of the imagery in *The Book of Visions* helpful for your own magical pathworkings.

Shamanism and the journey of the soul

Towards the end of Chapter One I referred to the American anthropologist and consciousness researcher Dr Michael Harner, who in recent years has played a major role in adapting the techniques of indigenous shamanism for a Western audience. These techniques are very relevant to anyone interested in visionary magic.

When I first became interested in shamanic visualisation, my initial response was that Harner's methods might not be compatible with Western magical practice. However, I soon discovered that this was not the case, for his method does not impose a belief system, only an operational procedure. Harner's approach to shamanic drumming and visualisation is valuable because it facilitates direct access to the visionary dimensions of the mind, and this means that the shamanic method can be used within any magical context. We have to remember that in a very real and profound sense the gods and goddesses are within us all, for they are the archetypal personifications of our spiritual potential. Michael Harner's approach to shamanic visualisation shows us how we may encounter these sacred archetypal god-forms within the visionary realm of inner space.

Harner usually holds his shamanic workshops in city tenement buildings or in large lecture rooms on different university campus sites, and has also trained numerous shamanic facilitators to continue this work both within the United States and internationally. His workshops feature the beating of a large, flat drum within a ritual context, and participants learn to explore ways of travelling on the drumbeat into the magical world for purposes of healing and self-exploration. Most of his workshop participants are already familiar with the concept of the shamanic visionary journey – traditionally known as the 'journey of the soul' – and the idea of 'riding' a rhythmic drumbeat into a state of meditative trance.

Harner's sessions begin as he shakes a gourd rattle to the four quarters in nearly total darkness, summoning the surrounding 'spirits' to participate in the shamanic working. He also encourages his group members to sing native shamanic chants and to enter into the process of engaging with the mythic world. His techniques include journeying in the mind's eye down the root system of an archetypal 'cosmic tree' or up imagined smoke tunnels into the sky. As the group participants delve deeper into a state of trance, assisted all the time by the drumming, they enter the 'mythic dreamtime' of their own unconscious minds, frequently having visionary encounters with a variety of animal and humanoid beings and perhaps also exploring unfamiliar locales. They may also make contact with spirit-allies or 'power animals'. Harner's approach is to show his participants that they can discover an authentic mythic universe within the depths of their own being.

The shamanic model of the Universe

In the core shamanic model that Harner presents, humanity is said to dwell on Middle Earth. Two other magical domains – referred to simply as the upper and lower worlds – may then be accessed through the shamanic trance journey. Often the upper and lower worlds appear to merge into a single magical reality which parallels the familiar world but which also seems to extend beyond it. The shaman seeks his spirit-allies as a way of obtaining new sources of vitality and sacred knowledge. The core intent is one of personal growth and healing, with many individual participants feeling that they have extended the boundaries of their awareness and their being.

Sometimes during these drum-journeys one gains a sense of the extraordinary range of mythological images which become available through the shamanic process. For example, one woman in a Harner workshop ventured to the upper world and had a remarkable 'rebirth' experience:

I was flying. I went up into black sky – there were so many stars – and then I went into an area that was like a whirlwind. I could still see the stars and I was turning a lot, and my power animals were with me. Then I came up through a layer of clouds and met my teacher – she was a woman I'd seen before. She was dressed in a long, long gown and I wanted to ask her how I could continue with my shamanic work, how to make it more a part of my daily life. Then she took me into her, into her belly. I could feel her get pregnant with me and felt her belly stretching. I felt myself inside her. I also felt her put her hands on top of her belly and how large it was! She told me that I should stop breathing, that I should take my nourishment from her, and I could actually feel myself stop breathing. I felt a lot of warmth in my belly, as if it were coming into me, and then she stretched further and actually broke apart. Her belly broke apart and I came out of her, and I took it to mean that I needed to use less will in my work, and that I needed to trust her more and let that enter into my daily life. That was the end of my journey – the drum stopped and I came back at that point.'[7]

Harner believes that mythic experiences of this sort are common during the shamanic journey and reveal a dimension of consciousness rarely accessed in daily life. He says:

Simply by using the technique of drumming, people from time immemorial have been able to pass into these realms which are normally reserved for those approaching death, or for saints. These are the realms of the upper and lower world where one can get information to puzzling questions. This is the Dreamtime of the Australian Aboriginal, the 'mythic time' of the shaman. In this area, a person can obtain knowledge that rarely comes to other people.[8]

Learning the shamanic technique

I first met Michael Harner at a conference in 1980 and his lectures and workshops made an immediate impression on me. Harner is a large, friendly man with a dense grey-black beard and mischievous eyes, and he would chuckle when presenting the paradoxes of the shaman's universe. He told the assembled group about power animals and magical forces in Nature without at all attempting to present a logical rationale. He explained how, for the South American Jivaro Indians, an individual could only reach maturity if protected by special power allies that accompanied that person and provided vitality and purpose. He showed us how to meditate on the repetitive rhythm of a drumbeat and how to ride this rhythm into the inner world, journeying down the root system of the Cosmic Tree or through smoke tunnels into the sky. He asked us not to judge these events when they occurred to us but to consider them on their own terms. We were, he said, entering a shamanic mode of trance consciousness where *anything* could happen, and probably would. But just because we saw strange, surreal events unfolding before us, or mythic animals in unfamiliar locales, we should not recoil from this experience but should instead participate in the process of discovering a new visionary universe within ourselves.

Harner's shamanic technique was remarkably simple. After blessing the group with his rattles, he would start pounding his drum and encourage us to dance free-form around the room with our eyes half closed, attuning ourselves to any form of spontaneous expression that would flow through us.

After only a short time, many people adopted animal postures and forms, and began to express these in very individual ways. Some people became bears and lumbered slowly around the room. Others became snakes or lizards. There were several wild cats, the occasional elephant, and a variety of birds. I myself seemed to have an eagle-hawk ally as I winged around through the group.

Harner then asked us to lie down on the floor and close our eyes. He began drumming in a monotonous, steady rhythm to allow us to ride down into the shamanic underworld. Harner had explained to us that this was not an 'evil' domain but simply the 'reverse' of our familiar, day-to-day world – a place where a different kind of reality prevailed. The technique was to imagine yourself entering the trunk of a large tree through a door at its base. Perhaps there were steps inside, but soon one would see the roots leading down at an angle of around 45 degrees. Following the root-tunnel you then journeyed still further downwards all the time propelled and supported by the constancy of the drumming. Finally you would see a speck of light at the end of the tunnel. Gradually drawing towards it, you would pass through into the light and look around at the new surroundings. Various animals would pass by, but we were asked to look for one that presented itself to us four times. That animal was possibly our own magical ally. Perhaps we would engage in conversation with this creature, be shown new magical vistas or landscapes, fly in the air, or be given gifts or special knowledge.

After a full day of drumming and magical journeying, the climax, for me, came in the evening. Harner asked us to imagine entering a smoke tunnel either by wafting upwards on smoke from a campfire or by entering a fireplace and soaring towards the sky through a chimney. At some time or other a water bird would present itself as an ally, he said, to lift us still higher into the sky-world. Harner was keen to know whether any of us saw any 'geometric structures', although he didn't wish to elaborate on this in case his comments had the effect of programming us into a specific visionary experience. As it turned out, several people in the group had visions of geometric 'celestial' architecture.

The room was quite dark as Harner began to beat on his drum and I found it easy to visualise the fireplace in my living room at home. The following is a transcript of my magical journey, recorded soon afterwards.

I enter the fireplace and quickly shoot up the chimney into a lightish grey whirling cloud tunnel. Soon I am aware of my guardian – a pelican with a pink beak.

Mounting the pelican's back I ride higher with it into the smoke tunnel. In the distance I see a golden mountain rising in the mist ...

As we draw closer I see that, built on the top of the mountain, is a magnificent palace made of golden crystal, radiating lime-yellow light. I am told that this is the palace of the phoenix, and I then see that golden bird surmounting the edifice. It seems to be connected with my own power-hawk.

I feel awed and amazed by the beauty of this place, but the regal bird bids me welcome. Then the hawk comes forward and places a piece of golden crystal in my chest. I hold my breath deeply as I receive it, for it is a special gift.

The drum is still sounding, but soon Michael indicates with a specific drumbeat that we should return. However, I am still high in the sky and find it very hard to re-enter the smoke tunnel. When I finally do begin to return the heavens remain golden, and as I travel down into the tunnel I look up to see saint-like figures rimming the tunnel, farewelling me ...

This journey was a very awesome one for me. After returning to an awareness of the workshop location and the people around me, I initially found it very difficult to articulate my thoughts. I seemed lost for words but was anxious, nevertheless, to communicate a sense of the importance that the journey had had for me. I felt I had been in a very sacred space.

I later discovered that mythic and symbolic journeys of this kind were not unusual – indeed, the combination of magical visualisation and repetitive drumming made it comparatively easy for participants to achieve the sense of entering magical or sacred space.

Ever since the early 1980s, when I first began conducting my own shamanic drumming sessions at conferences and in small, private gatherings, I have been amazed at the way in which ordinary people can have quite extraordinary visionary encounters during their spirit-journeys. At the end of each drumming session, time is always put aside for sharing and recounting what has occurred, and the remarkable fact which emerges is that authentic shamanic episodes can be experienced by mainstream city-dwellers in a modern urban setting – in other words, by nearly all of us! Shamanic drumming is the most powerful technique of visionary magic that I am aware of. I have found that during my own shamanic sessions an extraordinary amount of personally significant archetypal material has emerged into conscious awareness – in my case, imagery relating specifically to Kabbalistic, Gnostic and magical processes.[9]

During one of my meetings with Michael Harner I asked him whether there was any justification in regarding the shaman's visionary journey as simply a matter of imagination. That is to say, how could we be sure that the mythic experience of the shaman was *really* real? Harner's response was illuminating:

> Imagination is a modern Western concept that is outside the realm of shamanism. 'Imagination' already pre-judges what is happening. I don't think it is imagination as we ordinarily understand it. I think we are entering something which, surprisingly, is universal – regardless of culture. Certainly people are influenced by their own history, their cultural and individual history. But we are beginning to discover a map of the upper and lower worlds, regardless of culture. For the shaman, what one sees – that's *real*. What one reads out of a book is second-hand information. But just like the scientist, the shaman depends upon first-hand observation to decide what's real. If you can't trust what you see yourself, then what can you trust?[10]

The future of magic

So where will our exploration of visionary magic take us as the new millennium unfolds? Speaking personally, I think that in the years ahead more and more people will turn away from conventional paths of religious expression and will celebrate instead the essential mystery of Nature and the wonderful world around us. Magic is both Life-affirming and Nature-affirming. It honours the cycles of the seasons, it honours the gods and goddesses of Creation, and it honours our own sacred connection with the Universe as a whole.

An increasing number of people are now beginning to trust their own intuitive responses, their own inner *knowing*, as they seek to find meaning and spiritual purpose in their lives. Magic invests all of Nature and all of Life with sacred potential. We are all transformed by the process of expanding our personal horizons, and magic helps bring this about.

In earlier times, the world of magic was associated primarily with superstition and folklore; magic itself seemed to belong to an earlier era. But not any more. I feel certain that magic is here to stay, and that popular interest in it will become even stronger with the passage of time.

Magic is an ongoing process of spiritual self-transformation. Magic shows us how to explore our own inner potential, and how we can share the fruits of that potential with others. It proposes a deep respect for Nature and her processes, and requires full acknowledgment of the paradox that while our modern Western culture may be dominated by information technology, our very existence on this Earth remains a profound mystery.

If we can lead positive and meaningful lives during our time here, if we can help to transform our familiar realities into sacred realities, and if we can use our visionary potential to make our own lives, and the lives of those around us, more fruitful, prosperous and well-intentioned, we will surely be helping to make our world a better place. Putting these principles into practice on a regular basis means engaging fully in *everyday magic*.

SUPPLEMENTARY TEXTS

Symbols of the elements

Removing Spirit, which is omnipresent, the four basic elements – Earth, Water, Fire and Air – are associated magically with the four directions, with different signs of the Zodiac, with different seasons, with different times of the day and with different mythological creatures, or 'elemental spirits.'

Earth
Direction: North
Zodiacal signs: Taurus, Virgo and Capricorn
Season: Winter
Time of day: Midnight
Elemental spirits: Gnomes

Water
Direction: West
Zodiacal signs: Cancer, Scorpio and Pisces
Season: Autumn
Time of day: Dusk
Elemental spirits: Undines

Fire
Direction: South
Zodiacal signs: Aries, Leo and Sagittarius
Season: Summer
Time of day: Noon
Elemental spirits: Salamanders

Air
Direction: East
Zodiacal signs: Gemini, Libra and Aquarius
Season: Spring
Time of day: Dawn
Elemental spirits: Sylphs

Table of magical correspondences

SYMBOLIC QUALITY	KABBALISTIC SPHERE	GODS AND GODDESSES
Transcendence Androgyne (Alchemy)	Kether	Uranus (Greek); Coelus (Roman); Aion/Abraxas (Gnostic);Divine
Great Father/ Wisdom	Chokmah	Kronos (Greek); Saturn (Roman); Ptah (Egyptian)
Great Mother/ Understanding	Binah	Demeter (Greek); Juno (Roman); Isis (Egyptian); Boann/Danu (Celtic)
Merciful Ruler	Chesed	Zeus (Greek); Jupiter (Roman)
Aggressive Ruler	Geburah	Aries (Greek); Mars (Roman); Dagda (Celtic)
Sacred Son/ Harmony Spiritual rebirth	Tiphareth	Helios (Greek); Apollo (Roman); Ra/Horus/Osaris (Egyptian); Lugh (Celtic); Jesus (Christian)
Love and Intuition (Norse) Hathor	Netzach	Aphrodite (Greek); Venus (Roman); (Egyptian); Freya
Intellect	Hod	Hermes (Greek); Mercury (Roman); Thoth (Egyptian); Ogma (Celtic)
Sexuality/ Fertility	Yesod	Artemis (Greek); Diana (Roman); Bast (Egyptian); Brigit/Rhiannon (Celtic)
Sacred Daughter/ Earth	Malkuth	Persephone (Greek); Proserpine (Roman); Shekinah (Kabbalah)

Music for magical visualisation

During the mid-1980s, as ambient electronic music became more widely available, I began to research different types of music suitable for magical visualisation and meditation. I was attracted to the ambient genre of music because it was very minimalistic and non-intrusive.

In my book *Music for Inner Space*, I presented the idea of identifying different selections of ambient music with the elements Earth, Water, Fire, Air and Spirit, since we often recognise these particular characteristics in different styles of music. I also thought this would be a useful correlation because the five elements are central to several mystical systems, including yoga, alchemy and the Western magical tradition. My belief was that it might be helpful to choose specific sequences of recorded ambient music – Earth music, Water music, Fire music, and so on – and then produce a series of composite tape-recordings for personal use as musical backgrounds, especially when working with Tarot pathworkings or visualisations based on specific elements (e.g. the Tattvas).

The qualities of music

Music is useful as a supplement to meditation and creative visualisation because of its capacity to stimulate feelings and associations. Some types of music have a calming, relaxing quality, while others are intense and dramatic, helping to sharpen the intellect or stimulate specific, well-formed images in the mind's eye. Some types of music instil a sense of harmony and balance, while other discordant forms might leave us restless, on edge or lacking resolution. Some forms of music may seem to us to be trivial or whimsical, while other musical compositions have an impact that is profound or inspiring.

When choosing selections of music for visualisation or meditation it is important that the music should be tested by the individual meditator to ensure that it evokes specific associations, so that, like an affirmation, it helps reinforce a particular focus or orientation. If the music and the visualisation are competing against each other, the value of the music is obviously diminished.

In practical terms, selections of music chosen for the element Spirit are usually suitable as generalised ambient backgrounds for relaxation and meditation. Such music is typically devoid of strong melodic content and leads us towards a state of consciousness expansion while also remaining gentle and reflective in quality. This is music which literally enhances our inner journey of the spirit.

A selection of music for meditation and relaxation

Music for Spirit
Aeoliah and Larkin, *Inner Sanctum* (Celestial Octaves)
Aeoliah and Mike Rowlnd, 'Twin Flames Rising' and 'We are One Light' from *The Reiki Effect* (Oreade)
Ash Ra, 'Ocean of Tenderness' from *New Age of Earth* (Virgin)
Harold Budd and Brian Eno, *The Pearl* (EG/Polygram)
Brian Eno, *Ambient One: Music for Airports* (EG/Polygram)
Harold Budd and Brian Eno, *Ambient Two: The Plateaux of Mirror* (EG/Polygram)
Harold Budd, *The Room* (Atlantic)

Deuter, *Garden of the Gods* (New Earth)
Deuter, 'Green Mandala' and 'White Bird, Blue Sky' from *Sun Spirit* (New Earth)
Steven Halpern, *Eventide* (Halpern Music); *Zodiac Suite* (Halpern Music)
Nancy Hennings and Henry Wolff, *Tibetan Bells* and *Tibetan Bells II* (Celestial Harmonies)
Iasos, *Angelic Music* (Bluestar Communications)
Japetus, *The Radiant Self* (Listen Music) *Visions of Paradise* (Listen Music)
Gyorgy Ligeti, 'Requiem' and 'Lux Aeterna' from the *2001* soundtrack (MGM)
Ray Lynch, *The Sky of Mind* (Windham Hill)

A selection of music for magical visualisation

Music for Earth
Deuter, *Ecstasy* (Kuckuk)
Brian Eno, *Ambient Four: On Land* (EG/Polygram)
Steven Halpern, *Deja Blues* (Halpern Music)
Kitaro, *Oasis* (Kuckuk), 'Harmony of the Forest' from *Thinking of You* (Domo)

Music for Water
Harold Budd and Brian Eno, *Ambient Two: The Plateaux of Mirror* (EG/Polygram)
Brian Eno, *Thursday Afternoon* (EG/Polygram)
Larkin, *O'cean* (Wind Sung Sounds)
Pink Floyd, 'Echoes' from *Meddle* (Harvest /EMI)
Fripp and Eno, *Evening Star* (Island)
Edgar Froese, *Aqua* (Virgin)

Music for Fire
Ash Ra, 'Sun Rain' from *New Age of Earth* (Virgin)
Philip Glass, 'The Grid' from *Koyaanisqatsi* (Island)
Laraaji, *Ambient Three: Day of Radiance* (EG/Polygram)

Music for Air
Brian Eno, 'Under Stars' and 'Weightless' from *Apollo*
    (EG/Polygram)
Fripp and Eno, 'Wind on Water' and 'Wind on Wind'
    from *Evening Star* (Island)
Paul Horn, *Inside the Great Pyramid* (Mushroom)

The Book of Visions:
Pathways of the Tarot

The Major Arcana Tarot cards are like doorways to the mind and offer access to the symbolic paths which the magician follows on the inner journey of visionary exploration. Here is a description of that magical adventure, presented in the form of a continuous journey from the first pathway of *The World* through to the final pathway, *The Fool*. We are reminded that in the normal use of the word, a 'fool' is a person who knows nothing. However, in the magical tradition the person who knows *no-thing* has reached a state of transcendental spiritual awareness which embraces the infinity of Oneness – or Unity Consciousness – for Oneness takes us beyond individual forms and images. So, through an intriguing shift of emphasis and a symbolic play on words, *The Fool* is considered the supreme card in the Major Arcana – the path which leads to enlightenment through the awareness that ultimately all is One, and that Oneness knows no limits.

The Book of Visions describes the mystical journey which leads towards spiritual transcendence. Although this text is presented as a magical adventure, and is written in past tense, rather like a personal recollection of a highly symbolic dream, you may find it helpful to draw upon this imagery for your own magical visualisations and pathworkings.

I

While walking in the wooded hills, I came to a field of soft green grass beneath open blue sky. A light breeze rustled gently through the trees and birds were singing in the branches, and I felt a sense of deep tranquillity as I reflected on the special qualities of everything around me. But then, as I sat quietly in that place – an inspirational place which seemed at that moment to be so timeless and perfect – I remembered that everything which lives must also die. Mother Nature has her cycles of birth and death. Plants grow from seed, blossom into maturity and then pass from life into dust as new growth rises up to take their place.

As I rose to leave I realised that I too was journeying now towards my own death, and I wondered whether my journey would also take me towards new life. I continued on my way but perhaps ventured unintentionally down an unknown track, for I soon found myself in an unfamiliar part of the countryside.

I had come to a rocky cliff-face, hard and worn with time. I had always looked upon the texture of granite as a symbol of permanence, as something that would continue, impervious to change, for all the ages to come. But now I noticed that there were small rifts and channels in the rock, like wrinkles on the face of an old man. Suddenly these fissures in the rock appeared to open, becoming a doorway, and I was called to enter – though I knew not who had summoned me. Nevertheless, the call for me to enter was insistent, and the urge to explore undeniable. So now I continued cautiously on my way, passing deep into the earth, wondering where this exploration would take me.

The earthy passage I had entered was dark and moist, and yet it seemed to welcome me. All around, I sensed that unseen forces and powers were at work within the earth – sustaining all the living things growing in the soil, helping them reach up to the sun-drenched sky above.

Soon I became aware of an ethereal glow at the end of my path and I knew now that I had come to a large cave, deep below the earth. A misty, greeny-brown light played on the walls of the cave and I saw for the first time that, in the flickerings of soft light, a young maiden was dancing.

She was naked and beautiful and yet her body seemed to take many different forms. As if in a mirror, I saw within her dancing form vast fields of ripened wheat, and for a fleeting moment golden light shone from her face. But then she darkened, hardening into rock, and became completely impenetrable. And yet, even as I watched, an arc of pure water now flowed across her granite form, dissolving her hardness, and soon she had transformed into a country stream carrying grains of fine sand in its flow. And now she was dancing once again, a soft breeze uplfiting her golden hair.

As she danced, she called out to me, saying that she was dancing the endless story of life and death, and that she would teach me through her movements the motions of the world itself. And soon she had become the very essence of cyclic rhythm itself, for there was no constancy, no quiet or still point within her sensual movements.

Now she called me again, embracing me with her currents of energy, and I danced with her too, for I could do nothing else. As we embraced, a circle of misty light came up around us and it seemed that we were dancing in the dawn of the first days of the world. I was filled with joy, for I knew then that she and I were one, even though I had forgotten her all these long days past.

But then the mist became more dense and I could no longer see her. I called out to her, but when the mist finally subsided I could see that I was now alone. The maiden of the wondrous dance had disappeared.

I stood upon a rocky crag looking around, wondering where she had gone. And then a light breeze swept my face and I heard her voice once again: 'I am in the world,' she was telling me, in soft words which swept over me like music, 'but I am also beyond the sky. Follow the path. We will meet again, and we will dance once more together, but when we next meet you will have travelled an entire universe.'

II

As I walked on it seemed that I was now approaching the end of a tunnel. A radiant light enticed me onwards and then for the first time I heard the sudden blast of a trumpet, rich and full – a glorious sound which seemed to herald an awakening. Waves of pure music flowed through me and I was drawn along through darkness with the promise of light ahead.

Now I came into a strange and unfamiliar land, and there were others here as well. They were holding their hands up to the sky as if a marvellous portent was imminent. Men, women and children were here, side by side, waiting for what was to yet to unfold.

Suddenly the entire universe was ablaze with sound, and the waves of regal music which I had heard before now resounded once again. I was awed by the grandeur of this noble music as it filled my body with vibrant energy, and it seemed then that new life had awakened within me.

Then, suddenly, I was lifted high up in the air, embraced by a mass of swirling orange clouds. A new sense of exultation swept over me and I heard the voice of the clouds and the sky welcoming me to the heavens: 'Part of you has been left behind,' the orange clouds were telling me, 'but another part of you lies ahead. When you rediscover that forgotten part of your being, you will know then that your living has been like dying – and you must now regain what was yours a long time ago.'

III

The Moon . . .

I came now to a mighty castle flanked on three sides by the the waters of fate and possibility. As I watched, a crustacean came forth cautiously from the waters, with its ancient armour and its fierce claws. Then I noticed two animals upon a bank beside the castle. One of these was a wolf, its fur shaggy and unkempt, its expression hostile and aggressive. Beside it stood a domestic dog, tame and mild in manner, no longer dependent on wild prey for its survival but instead a friend of humanity.

Beyond them in the distance the formidable castle reached up towards the stars, its turrets rending the night sky. High up in the heavens the silvery moon cast her gaze down upon the waters. And all the while the Lord of the Castle stood in his turret, fortifying himself for an assault on the heavens, at odds with the natural forces beyond his castle walls.

I realised then that, like the lobster with its protective coverings, man forges the armoury of his own advancement, even though his armour is so often a barrier to the light. I also sensed that in journeying beyond the Castle of the Moon I would finally reach the central Sun, herald of the light of new dawn. Again I heard the call of the dancing maiden, urging me to continue on my way.

IV

The path ahead led to the foot of an impressive, grass-covered mountain. Halfway up the slope a rocky wall encircled the peak, enclosing the higher reaches of the sacred mountain which I knew would be barred to all except those who were pure of heart.

High up in the sky a glorious cosmic sun cast its radiance to all corners of the sky. It was shining also upon two young children who were dancing naked in a circle upon the grass of the lower slopes. They were holding hands in innocent celebration and seemed to bring down into their dancing the very essence of the sun itself.

I noticed that certain lessons had been inscribed upon the rocky wall, and these were five in number. The first lesson was that of seeing the world as it really is. The next was a lesson of hearing things as they really are, and there followed further lessons of the other senses: touch, smell and taste. And I knew then that beyond the world of sensory impressions there lay another world of spiritual awareness – a world which the gods and goddesses would keep sacred and free from profanity.

I could tell that these children understood this instinctively, for there was joy in their hearts. They knew that one day they would be granted entry to the higher slopes upon the holy mountain, and that here they would be reunited once again with the gods and goddesses of the sacred realms.

V

Now I ventured into a fertile, grassy valley illumined by bright stars shining in the clear night sky. To my great surprise I saw a beautiful naked maiden kneeling beside a stream. She held two vessels in her hands, one of gold and the other of silver, and she was using her vessels to collect the sacred waters of life from the stars in the night sky, and then pour this life-sustaining water down upon the earth.

I watched in awe as with her uplifted hand she captured the life-essence from the stars of light, and I saw that her vessel would never be emptied – for clearly she was the Priestess of the Eternal Waters and this was her sacred domain.

And I saw then that her whole body was shimmering with pale silver light and her flowing hair was like the current in the stream. I noticed too that there were eight stars shining in the night sky, one of them golden and brighter than the others. The star-maiden told me she would share with me her most prized secret, and reaching up into the sky she now used her golden vessel to capture the brilliance of the brightest star. Then she knelt, pouring its fluids upon the earth. And it seemed to me then that the whole world burst into life at this precious moment, even though most people were asleep and unaware of this miracle in their midst.

VI

I continued on my way, uplifted by the waters of life which had been bestowed on me by the maiden of the stream. But now the night sky, with its radiant stars, began to cloud over and I sensed an impending storm. A threatening darkness soon engulfed me, and it seemed that the whole universe had suddenly become hostile and uncertain.

Ahead in the grey light I saw a tall and weathered stone tower reaching up into the sky, but now this tower was threatened by the storm. Then, without warning, the heavens appeared to heave wide open and a molten torrent of thunder and lightning hurled itself wrathfully upon the vulnerable tower. Huge segments of stone masonry crashed heavily to the ground, battlements collapsed meekly before the onslaught, and soon the whole edifice was consumed by an enormous tongue of flame.

Then I understood all too clearly that there are forces and powers far in excess of man's modest achievements. And it seemed clear to me that anyone who sought to build a tower reaching up towards the heavens would have to construct it with noble intent – as an offering to the gods on high and not as a monument to human pride and vanity.

VII

Continuing on my path within the murky depths of the night, I came now to a poorly illumined cave. As I entered, it seemed that I was descending into the very bowels of the earth, and I felt increasingly overcome by a profound sense of despair, for my pathway was no longer clear.

I sensed other human presences, although their shapes were hard to discern, and now my attention focused on a crude splinter torch, the flickering flame of which cast large, distorted shadows upon the wall.

I saw now that the torch was held by a grotesque and bestial figure. Threatening, misshapen horns protruded from his skull, and I could see that abject decadence and innate evil had permanently etched their scars upon his distorted, leathery face. A few strands of fur hung down from his drooling lips, and his eyes were like burning coals, without pupils. An inverted pentagram was etched upon his forehead.

Standing before him were two semi-human naked figures, one male and the other female, clad only in chains. Horns had developed like growths from their heads, and the lower half of their bodies was thick-set and bovine. They were chained by their own self-pity and ignorance to the dark throne on which this horned god now held pride of place.

Then the dark god spoke to me, saying that his domain was the last outpost of humankind and that he took pleasure in encouraging those who found indulgent satisfaction in sensory delights.

He offered me a special place in his kingdom, pretending that his minions were in no way bound to remain in his service. I refused, demanding passage from his cave. He smiled benignly, disbelieving my determination as I repeated my request. Then, extending his arm, he held his torch aloft so I could draw near to see his face.

'Be not afraid,' he said, 'for even the Devil is another form of Light.' I drew even closer to his ugly, distorted face and looked searchingly into his dark, bottomless eyes. And then, from within the depths of his body, there came forth rays of white light, increasing in intensity.

Soon his head was ablaze with luminosity. His outline was no longer discernible, his grasp no longer apparent. I travelled past his glowing head as if passing through a doorway, and looking backwards at that moment it seemed to me that his bizarre form was nothing other than a monstrous pretence, for his very existence was founded in illusion.

I looked back again but now no demonic shapes whatever could be seen – only an unyielding rocky surface with no visible entrance to any subterranean cave.

I felt triumphant, and overcome with joy. The darkness had subsided, and I felt certain that new light was dawning.

VIII

But in this hope I was mistaken, for the landscape once again took on a strange and menacing aspect. The sun had risen above the horizon but the sky itself was now ablaze with blood and I saw that I had chanced upon a ploughed field strewn like a place of battle and torment with a vast amount of human carnage.

A vile and monstrous skeleton-god was striding up and down across the field with a commanding and persevering manner. In his hand he held a large sickle, its sharp metallic blade glinting menacingly in the sun.

I was alarmed to see that his crop was of human heads and limbs, and that they seemed to emerge from the soil to produce a macabre harvest. This was clearly the appointed time for him to reap the crop, and as his angry blade sang through the air, the heads of kings and commoners alike toppled and rolled along the ground.

The skeleton-god seemed impervious to the rights or wrongs of his vengeful task and continued with his fierce, downsweeping motions, wielding his terrible weapon in all corners of the field. Lying in the amber light, the fractured heads and limbs mocked the passive dignity of the nearby river, which seemed to flow in the direction of the rising sun. And still the reaper continued with his neverending task of death.

But then the strange skeleton creature turned and spoke to me. 'I am Death the first,' he said, 'but not Death the last. Those who come here no longer need their old, worn-out identities. It matters not who they were when they began their journey, for they are simply memories from former times. I help them move forward through death, so they may dwell in the sun ...'

The skeleton-god now motioned to me that I should make my way towards the river, and as I did so I saw that it was filled with golden light. Then he told me that I must journey in unison with the river, and allow myself to be swept along by its current – for this would then become a journey of light meeting light.

IX

And so I was borne along by the sparkling, golden river in the direction of new light and as I was swept on its current I noticed that one side of the stream fell away into darkness while the other was illumined by the light of the sun. And then I saw that the stream had a guardian, and he had a most imposing form – for he was sheathed in radiance, and majestic orange and blue drapes flowed from his shoulders.

In his right hand he held a water vessel, and in his left a glowing torch. At first I could not see his face, for it was shining with dazzling golden light, and my attention was drawn instead to the motifs inscribed upon his breastplate. Soon I discovered the image of the sun – source of all life and light – and then I saw that all the stars and constellations of the heavens were present here as well.

Then I saw that the guardian of the sacred stream was the overlord of two companion creatures, and I was given their names, for they were the red lion of the Sun and the silver eagle of the Moon.

The guardian now reached down towards the stream, and gathering some water with his cup he poured a spray of crystal droplets over the head of the lion. Then he lowered his torch over the head of the eagle. And it seemed for a moment that the eagle's body was made of glass, for as I watched a spark of flame fell down into the eagle's heart and filled its translucent body with a gentle, golden light.

'I am Raphael,' said the figure, addressing me at last. 'I guard the secrets of the sacred stream and the rainbow in the sky above.' Raphael told me then that I should continue on my way and travel towards a mountain with two commanding peaks, which were now visible on the horizon. Through these twin peaks I could see the pinky-golden rays of the rising sun illuminating the mountain slopes and heralding the arrival of the new day ahead.

X

But yet again I was mistaken, for as I came closer to the mountain the light seemed to recede and I was cast once more into darkness. The terrain here was barren and unwelcoming but I felt I had no choice but to venture onwards, although I was now unsure of my direction. Nevertheless, I felt a sense of reassurance, for in greater measure than before I now felt stronger and more assured within myself. Somehow I would have to find a guiding light to assist me on the rocky mountain path.

Then I realised that I was no longer alone. Quite suddenly I saw once again that I had a guide. He was robed in the grey tones of half-light, and stood high up upon a mountain ridge. He was looking down towards me, holding aloft a lantern illumined by a star from the night sky. In his other hand he carried a wooden staff, to help him maintain his balance on the precarious mountain path. He called down to me, asking me to come to him, and his voice was rich and deep – rich with the music of the valleys and the mountains.

As I drew closer I noticed that his face was partially concealed by a large hood, but his beard and his hair were as white as parched rock. I felt that I had seen him before, but as I gazed beneath his hood I saw not a face but an ocean. Soon there was no image there at all, but only my own reflection in the waters. I saw my own eyes in his, and my own face where his had been.

'I am your father and you are my son,' he told me, 'but also we are each other. You had forgotten, so I brought you here in order that you might remember.' The light from his lantern poured into me like a warm healing balm, as he continued. 'This,' he said, pointing to his lantern, 'is your lantern too, and you have been guiding yourself. And soon you will meet your true self – not in the dark meanderings of this mountain path, but in a place of light beyond light. And then you will know truly who you are, and where you have come from.'

XI

And now, as my robed and hooded guide merged back into the darkness of the mountain, I came into the presence of someone else whom I remembered. This was the maiden of the wheat field, the beautiful woman with whom I had danced when I began my journey. Now, however, she was more formally attired and her face was stern and impassive. She looked at me unsmilingly, her eyes searching my soul.

In the silken textures of her gown I saw once again the colours of grain swaying in the breeze. In her flowing cloak I discerned a molten fire which promised the welcoming heat of warmth but also the fire of destruction. I knew that her role was to judge my progress upon the journey so far, and that my fate, as from the beginning, lay entirely in her hands.

In her right hand, uplifted in a solemn and threatening gesture, the Goddess of Justice held a sturdy steel sword, and in her left, a pair of golden scales. 'I guard the secret of the sacred song,' she told me, 'and only a few prove worthy to hear it. This is the song which sounds throughout the Universe. This is the song through which all creatures live and breathe. But only some are destined to hear its melody as it calls them home ...'

As I watched, her eyes grew hard like the glistening steel of her sword, and her body became dense and impenetrable, like stone. There was no longer the spontaneity I recalled from our earlier time together, but instead a sense of enduring impartiality and sternness which overwhelmed me with awe.

Now the goddess held out her sword and rested its blade upon my head – a blade menacing in its presence and yet light and true in its touch. I saw my image reflected in one of her golden scales and watched tremulously as she placed a feather in the other. And I knew that either I would be permitted to pass or else she would bar my passage with all the strength and conviction of her authority.

Now I heard a rustling in the curtains behind her, and once again I saw within the folds of her silken gown images of the meadows and our first dance together. There was now warmth in her presence once again, and I knew that I had been spared her wrath.

She told me I would be given a song, and then I heard it for the first time – a reverberating echo which gradually quickened in pace and soon became a wave of ecstatic, heavenly music. And then I swam in the life-song of the gods, a song which seemed to echo through the infinite pathways of the Universe. Its splendour was overwhelming, its conception rich and overflowing with grace. And now it became more mellow, scaling down from a flow of wondrous harmonies to a single melody. This was my melody, my song ...

Now the gods were calling me, and I knew I could go still further upon my journey to the land of the Ancient Ones. Now they were calling me to return, and I knew I was welcome in their sacred terrain.

XII

I came now to a place where the air seemed tenuous and moist – a watery domain illumined by soft light which seemed to float down from the highest spheres of the heavens above.

And now as I looked up into the watery sky above me I saw something quite remarkable: a man hanging upside down like a reflection in a mirror. This was no ordinary human, for one of his legs was crossed over the other, and his arms were held behind his back. His very presence was like an omen from the gods.

Then, as I watched, a powerful light descended into his head and now it glowed like a beacon. For a moment I was immersed in a sea of light, thronging with different forms and endless possibilities.

I knew then that this figure was like a bridge between the lights of heaven and the subliminal oceans of being, and that I myself had come into existence from within these infinite depths. I knew too that if I could venture ever upwards, I would arrive finally at the ocean beyond all oceans, the ocean of Spirit itself.

And now the hanging man seemed ancient beyond all time. His fair, flowing hair had become hoary with age, his fine handsome face weathered by the currents and tides of the passing years. Wrinkles now lined his face, but still his eyes glowed with the wisdom of the gods.

Now he spoke to me with kindness and warmth, and his face once again became a beacon. And there was darkness no longer within the fabric of the waters.

XIII

I came at last to the gateway which serves as the entrance to the land of the great gods. And on this gateway was a mighty disc which some have called the Wheel of Fortune.

The wheel itself had been fashioned from cosmic fire, and as it revolved, great pulses of flame would issue from its rim. And I knew that this was how the stars and planets and constellations had come to be, in timeless aeons past.

No hand, it seemed, moved this wheel, and yet its motion was profound. Eight golden spokes supported the fiery rim and there were sacred guardians within its precincts.

At the cardinal points I saw the red lion and the silver eagle, the tawny bull and the face of the first and last man. And guarding the wheel as it rotated upon its axis was the ancient jackal god whom the Egyptians knew as Anubis and whom the ancient Greeks revered as a form of Hermes, messenger of the gods.

Beneath the gaze of Anubis, nations and peoples were born and rose only to die and fade from memory with the turning of the wheel. Continents and cultures rose to prominence and then were no more. Ideas once valued became lost or neglected. But I saw that always the journey of humankind continued, and this in itself was a source of great joy and inspiration. For the ancient gods and goddesses knew that with the passing of time, all living creatures would fulfil their destiny and make their way home.

XIV

Now I had come to a grassy plain where once again the sun was shining and the sky was golden yellow. In the distance I could see two forms – one human, the other animal – and as I drew nearer I could see them more clearly.

One was the maiden of the dance whom I had encountered more recently as the Goddess of Justice. This time her hair was once again the colour of golden grain and around her forehead was a garland of beautiful wild flowers. But to my amazement I saw that she was accompanied by the red lion of the Sun. And the maiden was now placing a wreath of white roses aound its neck to show that the lion too had become a symbol of peace.

And then a song came forth from the lion's mouth and it was the song of all wild animals the world over. It told of the time when man strode through the wilderness in the first days of his rule and how he had sought to quell the animal kingdom through his might and his cunning. How man himself had become the lord of the animals and how untrammelled strength and ferocity had then become the hallmark of his existence.

But when the maiden had heard this song she whispered gently to the lion, and caressed him, and she was telling him that now there was another way – that the power of love would always overcome the power of brute force. And this was her message: that with the white rose of peace one could overcome the red lion of fire.

XV

I continued my journey across the grassy plain and now I could see that the sky had changed from golden yellow to regal blue. The air had also become heavy with droplets of exquisite dew, and these shimmered in the air like a sheen of silver crystal. And although it was still daytime, everything around me now bore the mantle of the night.

I began to enter a region of swirling mists and I wondered who dwelt here as guardian of the sanctuary beyond. Then a golden light appeared from within the strands of mist, and soon this light became so dazzling that I had to shield my eyes.

A powerful voice now echoed through the mist, and it was the voice of one whose authority would remain unchallenged: 'I am the guardian of the chariot,' the voice told me, 'and I will take you now to the sacred places. On this journey great mysteries will be shown to you, but first you must prove that you are worthy to receive them.'

I felt both awe and apprehension, for I knew then that I was entirely at the mercy of a mighty warrior. And yet I knew also that in this domain I could depend forthrightly upon his strength and direction if my spiritual purpose was noble – for he was both the guardian of the heavens and a warrior of the Spirit.

I saw that the Charioteer was adorned in golden armour and that he wore an orange crown surmounted with the image of a sea crab. His hair glistened like pale shimmering fire and reached down to his shoulders, which were emblazoned with the insignia of the Moon. Around his waist was a band which told the legends of the planets and the stars, and the gods and goddesses who ruled over them.

The Charioteer held golden reins, and these in turn harnessed two sky-horses, one black, the other white. With these sky-horses he could travel in his cosmic chariot to the furthest corners of the universe. The chariot itself was embellished with a canopy of silver stars, supported by four columns of golden crystal. And the wheels of the chariot were like zodiacs, swirling through the night sky. As we journeyed swiftly through the heavens, it seemed to me that new worlds and life-forms burst into being in our wake.

And now we were flying towards the land of the Ancient Ones – the guardians of Time itself – those who knew its secrets and protected its mysteries.

XVI

We came down through the mist and alighted upon the grassy verges of a great mountain, and I knew that I had stood on this slope before.

Now as I looked down into the valley beyond I could see once again the rocky wall dividing the everyday world from the sacred terrain of the gods and goddesses. And I remembered that this was where I had seen two young children dancing in the grass beneath the sun.

Now these children had grown to adulthood, but their innocence and their purity were with them still. And still they were naked in this beautiful, unsullied paradise upon the slopes of the sacred mountain.

The young man was strong and handsome, and the light of sacred knowing shone from his face. Here upon this sacred land he was guardian of twelve eternal fires which glowed like luminous orbs – and these were the fires of the twelve palaces of the Zodiac.

His partner was graceful and beautiful, a maiden in the full flower of youth and innocence. Beyond her I could see the sacred Tree of Knowledge rising up into the golden orange sky, and the coiled serpent of wisdom had twined itself around the Tree.

These were the eternal lovers whose tenderness and caring had brought them together in sublime and innocent union. I knew that she was Eve, and he was Adam Kadmon – the first man – and that they would come to represent the aspirations and hopes of all of humanity.

Then above them, from within a haze of golden radiance, an angelic presence filled the sky. This was their protector, Gabriel. And Gabriel spoke, saying: 'These children are in my care, for they celebrate the love and wisdom of the Spirit. This land must forever remain a place of sanctuary and purity, for it is sacred to the Holy Ones.'

XVII

Now I came before the first of the mighty gods and goddesses, the great teacher known through all the ages as the Hierophant, Guardian of the Mysteries. He was seated upon a throne carved from the earth, and his throne had been placed between two pillars, one called Wisdom and the other, Beauty. And I knew that he would only share his knowledge with those who were worthy to receive.

I dared not look upon his face, but I saw that his robe, which flowed down to the ground before me, was flame-red like molten lava, and that upon his breast he wore a silver pentagram to celebrate the five elements – the greatest of which is Spirit. In his left hand he held a golden staff, and in his right the sacred keys which unlock the Mysteries of the Sun and Moon.

Gaining courage, I now looked up and I saw that his face was of pure white light, and that upon his noble head was a triple-layered crown. And as I stood before him he began to sing, and I knew this to be the sacred song of the first days of the world. This was the song whose harmonies had given form to all living things within the Universe, and I knew then that the Hierophant was the true Lord of the Earth and that in him were all the secrets of the Divine Word made manifest.

Now he gestured towards the pentagram upon his breast, and I saw once more the silver star and the figure of the first human. But then I noticed in the centre of the pentagram my own face, and I knew that I too had received a name in the earliest times, and that this name was the true reason why I had come forth into the world. But I had forgotten the name which had been given to me, and I had come here once more to gain the knowledge of my true identity.

As I stood there the Hierophant held out his golden staff and placed it lightly upon my head. And now the music of the gods – a cascade of lilting, ethereal harmonies – echoed through my soul and I saw myself as I had travelled through all the ages, from death to birth to life, in a continuing cycle of becoming. A torrent of human images flowed before my eyes and I knew that these were the vestiges of my own being and existence which had been summoned back into the shadows by the Lord of the Earth when their time was nigh. And yet I knew too that my own being – my sacred and eternal being – was inviolate, for my soul was a gift of the Holy Ones.

Then the Hierophant spoke to me, telling me that my true name was my most precious possession, and that I must guard and remember it always. And then he passed me a silver pentagram that was mine and mine alone, and placed it upon my breast. Looking down at it, I marvelled at its silver radiance – the light of life – and I saw that in its centre was written my innermost and most prized secret, my true and sacred name.

XVIII

Continuing my journey, I came now to a range of wondrous and awe-inspiring mountains which seemed to have been carved from crystal fire by the forces of Time itself. For here were currents of flame, caught like thunderbolts in ice.

I knew that these mountains must have a ruler, and then I saw him – a ruler as ancient as the land itself, a ruler older than the first days of the world.

The Emperor of the Universe sat with passive dignity and noble presence upon a throne carved from red rock. From his crown flashed red and golden light and I saw that his armour was embossed with the symbols of the Sun.

The Emperor's armour was a gift from his warring brother, the Lord of the Chariot, who ruled the outer reaches of the Cosmos with a vengeful hand.

But the Emperor himself was a Lord of Peace, and here upon his throne he sat in untroubled silence, watching over his kingdom, subject as it was to the tides of eternal change. And to those within his kingdom who rose up from time to time in search of purpose and harmony, the Emperor would despatch beams of radiant light, and those particles of light would fall down upon the world as a blessing from the gods.

And yet the Emperor himself was the monarch of a quiet and barren land, for there was no goddess in his kingdom to bring life and abundance to this mountainous terrain. And it was said that through all the aeons past, the Emperor had yearned for the sweet Goddess of the Moon to cast her gaze upon his barren world and bless it with her touch.

So I felt an abiding sadness, for I knew that this Lord of the Mighty Ones was searching for a Queen to bring the waters of life into his kingdom and partner him as Goddess of the Moon. And yet it seemed destined that beyond these sacred mountains the

King and the Queen might yet find each other – that, in another time and place, they would one day be united.

XIX

Continuing on my way, I left the land of barren mountains behind me and came down into a fertile valley. Here there were vast fields of ripe golden wheat, and groves of regal and luxuriant trees. Along my pathway the earth was strewn with abundant wildflowers rejoicing in the sunlight, and I saw that a crystal river flowed through this valley, nourishing the rich, dark soil with its pure waters. As I drew closer, I realised I had come to the sacred domain of the Empress, Queen of Life and Light.

She was seated beside the river upon a throne of flowers, and a shimmering green cloak flowed down from her shoulders to the abundant earth around her. Her golden hair danced with beams of sunlight, and sweet roses grew at her feet. The colours which embellished her gown were all the colours of the four seasons and the timeless cycles of Nature. And beneath her foot lay a silver crescent moon.

As I looked upon her loving face I saw once again the beautiful maiden from my dance at the dawn of time. But then the Empress took another form, and now she was Mother of us both. And as I looked into her wise and welcoming eyes I felt very much a part of her – for I was truly of her essence – and I knew then that it was from her womb that I had first come forth into the world.

Then it seemed that the Empress became one with the crystal river, and the crystal river became one with the ocean – and the foam and cresting waves of the ocean were like a universal dance of all that was or ever could be. Upon every swirling arc of spray there were a thousand spiralling universes. And in every seashell upon every ocean beach I could hear the songs and stories from the infinite shores of time.

XX

And yet there was a time when the Queen of Life and Light had herself been young, when she herself had not yet taken her place as Empress upon the throne of flowers.

I came now to the temple of her younger days, when she was not yet the future Queen and partner of the King of the red mountains. Here she served as High Priestess of the Moon and sat enthroned between the twin pillars of night and day. And so it was that I came to visit her in her twilight world, a realm of shimmering silver light.

Her skin was as white as snow, but her eyes and mouth were hard like polished steel. From her shoulders flowed a cloak of water, blue-black like the depths of the ocean which even beams of sunlight have not reached.

Upon her lap lay unfurled the scroll of sacred memory, the book of deeds forgotten by humankind but recalled by gods and goddesses like reflections in a mirror. And I knew that in her scroll my true name had been written, a name which had been given to me as my most prized possession. But while the Hierophant had acknowledged me and given me my name, the High Priestess seemed not to heed me as I entered her court, and it was as if a veil of mist had come between us – a veil which made her seem distant and elusive.

I felt deserted by her coldness, shunned by her aloof manner. And yet there was a freshness in her presence and it seemed that I was walking on hallowed ground, for her temple was dedicated to the dawn of the world itself. Later I would realise that although the Sun King had come forth to rule from the mountains of fire, this High Priestess of the Moon had not yet ventured beyond the realm of sacred dreams. Still she dwelt within a temple of shadows, veiled by the misty twilight of the first dawn.

XXI

Beyond the veil of mist I now came to the realm of the Magician, master of Earth, Water, Fire and Air. A noble and awesome figure, his eyes were ablaze with lightning and his every footstep was like a roar of thunder. He held his right arm aloft to the heavens, summoning the mighty forces of the sky, and then with his left arm he despatched thunderbolts to the worlds below.

And yet, like the High Priestess of the Moon, he too was a guardian who dwelt beyond the veil of form. In him the Divine Word was still new, and had not yet found its voice in the language of the Ancient Ones.

This Lord of Magic had four symbols which were his sacred code.

When he showed me Earth I saw all the mountains and valleys which would become the backbone of the universe.

When he showed me Water I saw a cosmos emerging from an infinite ocean. All the thoughts and memories which could ever float into human dreams were written in these sacred waters.

When he showed me Fire I beheld the flame beyond flame, the luminosity within all blazing suns. And this was the light beyond light which illumined universes as yet undreamed of by the gods and goddesses.

And when he showed me Air I felt the sweet breath of life which would enter all things within the unfolding worlds of form, and which henceforth would be given to the watchful care of the Ancient Ones.

Then I saw that Earth, Water, Fire and Air, united as one, gave rise to a beautiful sacred song, and this was the Song of Spirit. And as this song flowed forth into all the worlds, all directions became one direction, all beauty one beauty. There was no division, but only a mighty and wondrous harmony.

The Magician told me then that it was through Earth, Water, Fire and Air that my soul of light had come to be, and my true name given. And so now I ventured still further upon my quest, to discover whence I had come.

XXII

I know I have come now to the last pathway on my journey to the Ancient Ones. I look around and I see that I have come to the edge of a mighty cliff, beyond which lies an infinite ocean – the ocean of infinite possiblity from which all things come forth.

I am alone and yet I am at peace. This is my home, for I have been here before. All around me I feel great warmth and love. I feel young again, renewed. I wear an inner jacket as white as snow, and my outer garments are embroidered with the sigils of the Sun. Upon my shoulder is an emblem of the Silver Moon and around my waist I wear a belt inscribed with the legends of the Zodiac. And in a small wallet which hangs from my belt are all the things which are mine in the world. These few possessions I have treasured on my journey, and yet I do not know the value of their worth. They are mementos which I have saved like coinage, and which in fond memory I carry with me now as a reminder of former times.

I take these few items from my wallet to esteem my wealth. But the Sun has caught them, and demands its spoils – my memories dissolve within the haze. And yet a new treasure is mine. The light is brighter now, and looking down upon the rocks at the cliff edge I notice a solitary red rose, glimmering like the deep fire in the eyes of the all-seeing gods. I stoop to pick it up, and place it in my wallet.

And all the time I feel the lure of the infinite ocean beyond form, which embraces me from all sides as I stand upon the ledge.

She is calling me. I hear the sweet voice of the maiden of the golden wheat fields, for her voice is in the sky. She is pleased that at last I have returned to her; she is happy I have come. And yet I cannot see her face, or glimpse her graceful dancing form.

I feel she is around me, all around me. I feel her love within me.

I hear her voice. We are together already. She is me and I am her.

We float out beyond the mountain into the infinite ocean of all being. And looking back I see another figure in imitation of myself, draped in the colours of the Sun and Moon. A Fool sitting upon the cliff edge – but I cannot see his face.

And now his wallet has fallen from his belt, and the red rose has spilled forth upon the rocks. Its petals have scattered in merry disarray and dance carefree in the air.

ENDNOTES

Introduction
1 Stanislav Grof (ed.), *Ancient Wisdom and Modern Science*, p. 10.
2 David Bohm, 'A New Theory of the Relationship of Mind and Matter', *The Journal of the American Society of Psychical Research*, vol. 80, no. 2, p. 126.
3 Danah Zohar, *The Quantum Self*, p. 106.

Magic, symbol and image in the magical universe
1 See Gershom Scholem, *Major Trends in Jewish Mysticism*, pp 215–16.
2 ibid., pp 218–19.
3 Quoted in H. Stanley Redgrove, *Alchemy: Ancient and Modern*, pp 10–11.
4 Quoted in M. Berthelot, *La Chimie au Moyen Age*, p. 262.
5 Redgrove, op. cit., p. 14.
6 For a full description of these initiations see Janet and Stewart Farrar, *The Witches' Way*.

7   Titus Burckhardt, *Alchemy*, Penguin Books, Baltimore 1971, p. 75.
8   Z. Budapest, *The Holy Book of Women's Mysteries*, p. 278.
9   N. Drury, *The Occult Experience*, p. 51.
10 Quoted in Victoria Williams, 'The Sacred Craft', *East West*, October, 1984.
11 See John G. Neihardt, *Black Elk Speaks*, p. 36.
12 Quoted in Eugene Stockton, *The Aboriginal Gift*, p. 82.
13 For further information see Michael Harner, *The Jivaro*.
14 Quoted in Joan Halifax (ed.), *Shamanic Voices*, p. 185.
15 ibid., p. 183.
16 See Michael Harner, *The Way of the Shaman*, p. 62.
17 ibid., p. 20.
18 See Robert G. Lake, 'Tela Donahue Lake: Traditional Yurok "Doctor"', *Shaman's Drum*, no. 15, mid-winter 1989, p. 47 et seq.
19 ibid.
20 See Ake Hultkrantz, 'The Wind River Shoshoni Sun Dance and Curing Practices', *Shaman's Drum*, no. 17, mid-summer 1989, p. 17 et seq.

First step on the visionary path

1   John Lilly, *Simulations of God*, p. 33.
2   For associations between the Tattva elements and the signs of the Zodiac, the seasons, the time of the day and various mythological creatures, see pp 169–70 of the Supplementary texts.
3   In Wicca these are sometimes known as the Guardians of the Watchtowers.

Sacred magic, everyday magic

1   Starhawk, *The Spiral Dance*, p. 72.
2   Readers may wish to refer to the various tables in Chapters

Two and Three, and also to the Table of Magical Correspondences at the back of this book (see p. 171).

3   Some magical rituals in the Golden Dawn tradition utilise the magic triangle, but this symbol has a very different meaning from the circle. Unlike the circle, which symbolises the Infinite, the triangle represents finite manifestation, a focus for that which already exists. Symbolic of the spiritual, mental and physical levels in all forms of creation, the triangle represents *evocation* – a magical term for calling forth specific spirit-beings by means of spells or words of power. The magical talisman placed in the centre of the triangle incorporates the seal or sign of the spirit and provides the focus of the ritual. Some ritual magicians have regarded the evoked spirits as their 'spirit familiars' or 'astral guard-ians'. Interested readers are referred to the practical writings and magical diaries of Aleister Crowley, and also Franz Bardon's seminal work, *The Practice of Magical Evocation.*

4   In the Golden Dawn the wand was originally ascribed to the element Fire, and the sword to the element Air, but as Francis King and Stephen Skinner point out in *Techniques of High Magic* (p. 60), it makes more sense to switch these symbolic associations.

5   James R. Lewis (ed.), *Magical Religion and Modern Witchcraft,* p. 100.

6   See Nevill Drury, *The History of Magic in the Modern Age,* p. 177.

7   It remains simplistic to think of magic in terms only of good and evil. For a more detailed perspective on the nature of how black magicians view their metaphysical path, readers are referred to my book *The History of Magic in the Modern Age.*

8   Some Wiccans invoke the Guardians of the Four Quarters by commencing in the north – the direction of the Pole Star – while others favour the east as the direction of the

rising sun. Here the Wiccan approach is to use the pentagram to invoke, by starting with tip of the five-pointed star
in each quarter and then completing the shape anti-clock-
wise, the reverse direction from that used in banishing. The
invocation is simple and direct: For example, 'O great Lord
of the North and the elemental power of Earth I invoke
your presence to protect this circle during the ritual I am
about to perform.' See Michael Howard, *Way of the
Magus*, p. 28.

9   Quoted in Zsuzsanna Budapest, *The Holy Book of Women's
     Mysteries*, p. 118.
10   Aidan Kelly, *Crafting the Art of Magic*, p. 52; and also
     Janet and Stewart Farrar *Eight Sabbats for Witches*.
11   Janet and Stewart Farrar, *Eight Sabbats for Witches*, pp.
     42–43.
12   Aleister Crowley, *Book Four*, p. 42.
13   For example, see Cassandra Eason, *A Complete Guide to
     Magic and Ritual*, and Zsuzsanna Budapest, *The Holy
     Book of Women's Mysteries*.
14   Budapest, op. cit., p. 223.
15   Elisabeth Brooke, *A Woman's Book of Shadows*, p. 205.

The magic of love and sexuality

1   Brandy Williams, *Ecstatic Ritual*, p. 96.
2   Francis King, *Tantra: The Way of Action*, pp 29, 44.
3   Carl Weschcke, introduction to Jonn Mumford, *Ecstasy
     Through Tantra*, pp xiv–xvi.
4   Mumford, op. cit., p. 31.
5   Swami Sivananda Sarasvati, 'Shakti-Yoga Philosophy', in
     Swami Sivananda Radha, *Kundalini Yoga for the West*,
     pp 25–28.
6   Haridas Chaudhuri, 'Yoga Psychology', in Charles Tart
     (ed.), *Transpersonal Psychologies*.
7   King, op. cit., pp 116–117.

8   Williams, op. cit., pp 21–22.
9   ibid., p. 16.

Visionary magic – a journey of self-discovery

1   John Lilly, *Simulations of God*, p. 33.
2   V. H. Soror, V.N.R., 'Of Skrying and Travelling in the Spirit-Vision', in Israel Regardie (ed.), *The Golden Dawn*, vol. 4, pp 29–42, reprinted in Francis King (ed.), *Astral Projection, Magic and Alchemy*.
3   King (ed.), op. cit., p. 69.
4   Quoted in Israel Regardie (ed.), op. cit., vol. 4, p. 43. The god-name HCOMA is not a Kabbalistic god-name but derives from an 'angelic language' called Enochian, transcribed by the Elizabethan occultists Dr John Dee and Edward Kelley and subsequently utilised in Golden Dawn rituals and visualisations.
5   A specific allusion to Golden Dawn 'Inner Order' levels of ritual attainment.
6   Quoted in King (ed.), op. cit., pp 58–59.
7   Personal communication during filming for the Cinetel Productions documentary *The Occult Experience*, New York, November 1984, in which I was involved as interviewer. This documentary, screened in Australia by Channel Ten and released in the United States through Sony Home Video, included a lengthy segment on this particular shamanic drumming workshop.
8   See Nevill Drury, *The Occult Experience*, p. 145.
9   Readers who are interested may wish to peruse my book *Vision Quest*, which describes some of my trance journeys using Michael Harner's shamanic drumbeat method.
10   Drury, *The Occult Experience*, loc. cit.

BIBLIOGRAPHY

Books on practical magic

Ashcroft-Nowicki, D., *First Steps in Ritual*, Aquarian Press, Wellingborough, 1982.

Ashcroft-Nowicki, D., *The Shining Paths: An Experiential Journey through the Tree of Life*, Aquarian Press, Wellingborough, 1983.

Ashcroft-Nowicki, D., *Highways of the Mind: The Art and History of Pathworking*, Aquarian Press, Wellingborough, 1987.

Bardon, F., *The Practice of Magical Evocation*, Rudolph Pravica, Graz-Puntigam, Austria, 1967.

Bowes, S., *Woman's Magic*, Piatkus, London, 1999.

Brooke, E., *A Woman's Book of Shadows*, The Women's Press, London, 1993.

Budapest, Z., *The Holy Book of Women's Mysteries*, Wingbow Press, Oakland, California, 1989.

Butler, W.E., *The Magician: His Training and Work*, Aquarian Press, London, 1959.

De Angeles, L., *Witchcraft: Theory and Practice*, Llewellyn, St Paul, Minnesota, 2001.

Eason, C., *A Complete Guide to Magic and Ritual*, Piatkus, London, 1999.

Farrar, J. & Farrar, S., *Eight Sabbats for Witches*, Robert Hale, London, 1981.

Farrar, J. & Farrar, S., *The Witches' Way*, Robert Hale, London, 1984.

Farrar, J. & Farrar, S., *The Witches' Bible*, Magickal Childe, New York, 1985.

Farrar, J. & Farrar, S., *The Witches' Goddess*, Robert Hale, London, 1987.

Farrar, S., *What Witches Do*, Phoenix, Custer, Washington, 1983.

Fortune, D., *The Mystical Qabalah*, Ernest Benn, London, 1957.

Gray, D., *How to be a Real Witch*, HarperCollins, Sydney, 2001.

Horne, F., *Witch*, Random House, Sydney, 1998.

Howard, M., *Way of the Magus*, Capall Bann Publishing, Berkshire, 1996.

King, F., & Skinner, S., *Techniques of High Magic: A Manual of Self-Initiation*, C.W. Daniel, London, 1977.

Knight, G., *A Practical Guide to Qabalistic Symbolism* (vols1 & 2), Helios, Cheltenham, 1965.

Mumford, J., *Ecstasy Through Tantra*, Llewellyn, St Paul, Minnesota, 1988.

Starhawk, *The Spiral Dance*, Harper & Row, New York, 1979.

Warren-Clarke, L., *The Way of the Goddess*, Prism Press, Dorset, 1987.

Williams, B., *Ecstatic Ritual*, Prism Press, Dorset, 1990.

General books on magic, mythology and the mystical traditions

Abraham, L., *A Dictionary of Alchemical Imagery*, Cambridge University Press, Cambridge, 1998.

Adler, M., *Drawing Down the Moon*, Beacon Press, Boston, 1988.

Alvarado, L., *Psychology, Astrology and Western Magic: Image and Myth in Self-Discovery*, Llewellyn, St Paul, Minnesota, 1991.

Ankarloo, B. & Clark, S. (eds), *Witchcraft and Magic in Europe: The Twentieth Century*, Athlone Press, London, 1999.

Berthelot, M., *La Chimie au Moyen Age*, Paris, 1893.

Bolen, J.S., *Goddesses in Everywoman*, Harper & Row, New York, 1985.

Bolen, J.S., *Gods in Everyman*, HarperCollins, New York, 1989.

Burckhardt, T., *Alchemy*, Penguin Books, Baltmore, 1971.

Campbell. J., *The Hero with a Thousand Faces*, Pantheon, New York, 1949.

Campbell. J., *Myths to Live By*, Viking Press, New York, 1972.

Campbell. J., *The Inner Reaches of Outer Space: Metaphor as Myth and as Religion*, Harper & Row, New York, 1988.

Case, P.F., *The Tarot*, Macoy Publishing Co., New York, 1947.

Castaneda, C., *The Teachings of Don Juan*, University of California Press, Berkeley, California, 1968.

Castaneda, C., *A Separate Reality*, Simon & Schuster, New York, 1971.

Castaneda, C., *Journey to Ixtlan*, Simon & Schuster, New York, 1972.

Castaneda, C., *Tales of Power*, Simon & Schuster, New York, 1974.

Castaneda, C., *The Art of Dreaming*, HarperCollins, New York, 1993.

Cavendish, R., *The Tarot*, Michael Joseph, London, 1973.

Chaudhuri, H., 'Yoga Psychology', in Tart, C. (ed.), *Transpersonal Psychologies*, Harper & Row, New York, 1975.

Crowley, A., *Magick in Theory and Practice*, privately published, Paris, 1929 (republished by Dover and Castle Books, New York, various editions).

Crowley, A., *Book Four*, Sangreal Foundation, Dallas, 1972.

Crowley, V., *A Woman's Kabbalah: Kabbalah for the 21st Century*, Thorsons, London, 2000.

Crowley, V., *Wicca: The Old Religion in the New Millennium*, Thorsons, London, 1996.

Crowther, P., *Lid off the Cauldron*, Muller, London, 1981.

Drury, N., *Vision Quest*, Prism Press, Dorset, 1984.

Drury, N., *Music for Inner Space,* Prism Press, Dorset, 1985.

Drury, N., *The Occult Experience*, Robert Hale, London, 1987.

Drury, N., *The Elements of Shamanism,* Element, Dorset, 1989.

Drury, N., *Exploring the Labyrinth: Making Sense of the New Spirituality*, Continuum, New York, 1999.

Drury, N., *The History of Magic in the Modern Age*, Constable, London, 2000.

Dyer, W., *Real Magic*, HarperCollins, New York, 1992.

Dyer, W., *Your Sacred Self*, HarperCollins, New York, 1995.

Edinger, E., *Ego and Archetype*, Penguin, London, 1973.

Eliade, M., *Shamanism*, Princeton University Press, New Jersey, 1972.

Eliade, M., Feinstein, D. & Krippner, S., *Personal Mythology*, Tarcher, Los Angeles, 1988.

Fisdel, S.A., *The Practice of Kabbalah*, Aronson, New Jersey, 1996.

Gettings, F., *The Book of Tarot*, Triune Books, London, 1973.

Getty, A., *A Sense of the Sacred*, Taylor Publishing, Dallas, 1997.

Gray, E., *A Complete Guide to the Tarot*, Crown, New York, 1973.

Gray, W.G., *Inner Traditions of Magic*, Weiser, Maine, 1984.

Green, M., *The Elements of Natural Magic*, Element Books, Dorset, 1989.

Greer, M.K., *Women of the Golden Dawn*, Park Street Press, Rochester, Vermont, 1995.

Grof, S. (ed.), *Ancient Wisdom and Modern Science*, State University of New York Press, Albany, 1984.

Halifax, J. (ed.), *Shamanic Voices*, Arkana, New York, 1991.

Harner, M., *The Way of the Shaman*, Harper & Row, San Francisco, 1980.

Harner, M., *The Jivaro*, University of California Press, Berkeley, 1984.

Harvey, G., *Listening People, Speaking Earth*, Hurst, London, 1997.

Hoffman, E., *The Heavenly Ladder: Kabbalistic Techniques for Inner Growth*, Prism Press, Dorset, 1996.

Houston, J., *The Search for the Beloved: Journeys in Sacred Psychology*, Crucible, Wellingborough, 1990.

Houston, J., *The Hero and the Goddess*, Ballantine, New York, 1992.

Houston, J., *A Passion for the Possible*, HarperCollins, San Francisco, 1997.

Howe, E., *The Magicians of the Golden Dawn*, Routledge & Kegan Paul, London, 1972.

Hutton, R., *The Triumph of the Moon: A History of Modern Pagan Witchcraft*, Oxford University Press, Oxford, 1999.

Jamal, M., *Shape Shifters*, Arkana, New York, London, 1987.

Jones, P. & Matthews, C. (eds), *Voices from the Circle*, Aquarian Press, London, 1990.

Jordan, M., *Witches: An Encyclopedia of Paganism and Magic*, Kyle Cathie, London, 1996.

Jung, C.G., *Symbols of Transformation*, Bollingen Foundation, New Jersey, 1956.

Jung, C.G., *Man and his Symbols*, Dell, New York, 1968.

Kalweit, H., *Dreamtime and Inner Space*, Shambhala, Boston, 1988.

Kaplan, A., *Meditation and Kabbalah*, Weiser, New York, 1982.

Kelly, A., *Crafting the Art of Magic*, Llewellyn, St Paul, Minnesota, 1991.

King, F. (ed.), *Astral Projection, Magic and Alchemy*, Spearman, London, 1971.

King, F. (ed.), *Tantra: The Way of Action*, Destiny Books, Rochester, Vermont, 1990.

Knaster, M., 'The Goddesses in Jean Shinoda Bolen', *East West*, March, 1989.

Levi, E., *The Key of the Mysteries*, Rider, London, 1959.

Lewis, J.R. (ed.), *Magical Religion and Modern Witchcraft*, State University of New York Press, Albany, 1996.

Lilly, J., *Simulations of God*, Simon & Schuster, New York, 1975.

Luhrmann, T.M., *Persuasions of the Witch's Craft*, Harvard University Press, Cambridge, Massachusetts, 1989.

Matt, D.C., *The Essential Kabbalah*, HarperCollins, New York, 1995.

Matthews, C. & Matthews, J., *The Western Way*, Arkana, London, 1994.

McKenna, T., *The Archaic Revival*, HarperCollins, San Francisco, 1991.

Metzner, R., *The Unfolding Self: Varieties of Transformative Experience*, Origin Press, Novato, California, 1998.

Moore, R., & Gillette, D., *King, Warrior, Magician, Lover*, HarperCollins, San Francisco, 1990.

Neihardt, J. G., *Black Elk Speaks*, Pocket Books, New York, 1972.

O'Hara, G., *Pagan Ways*, Llewellyn, St Paul, Minnesota, 1997.

Pearson, C.S., *The Hero Within*, HarperCollins, San Francisco, 1989.

Pearson, C.S., *Awakening the Heroes Within*, HarperCollins, San Francisco, 1991.

Radha, S.S., *Kundalini Yoga for the West*, Shambhala, Boulder, Colorado, 1981.

Redgrove, H.S., *Alchemy: Ancient and Modern*, Rider, London, 1922.

Regardie, I. (ed.), *The Tree of Life: A Study in Magic*, Rider, London, 1932.

Regardie, I. (ed.), *The Golden Dawn*, vols 1–4, Aries Press, Chicago, 1937–40.

Regardie, I. (ed.), *The Middle Pillar*, Aries Press, Chicago, 1945.

Regardie, I. (ed.), *The Philosopher's Stone*, Llewellyn, St Paul, Minnesota, 1970.

Richardson, A., *Priestess: The Life and Magic of Dion Fortune*, Aquarian Press, Wellingborough, 1987.

Scholem, G., *Major Trends in Jewish Mysticism*, Schocken, New York, 1961.

Scholem, G., *Origins of the Kabbalah*, Princeton University Press, New Jersey, 1990.

Scholem, G., *On the Mystical Shape of the Godhead*, Schocken, New York, 1997.

Shumaker, W., *The Occult Sciences in the Renaissance*, University of California Press, Berkeley, California, 1979.

Skelton, R., *Spellcraft*, Routledge & Kegan Paul, London, 1978.

Stockton, E., *The Aboriginal Gift*, Millennium, Sydney, 1995.

Tart, C. (ed.), *Transpersonal Psychologies*, Harper & Row, New York, 1975.

Valiente, D., *An ABC of Witchcraft, Past and Present*, Hale, London, 1973.

Valiente, D., *Witchcraft for Tomorrow*, Hale, London, 1978.

Waite, A.E., *The Holy Kabbalah*, University Books, New York, 1960.

Waite, A.E., *The Pictorial Key to the Tarot*, Weiser, New York, 1973.

Zohar, D., *The Quantum Self*, HarperCollins, London, 1991.

INDEX